FINANCIAL INSTITUTIONS AND SERVICES

FEDERAL INTERVENTIONS IN RESPONSE TO THE FINANCIAL CRISIS

A RETROSPECTIVE OF COSTS

FINANCIAL INSTITUTIONS AND SERVICES

Additional books in this series can be found on Nova's website under the Series tab.

Additional e-books in this series can be found on Nova's website under the eBooks tab.

FINANCIAL INSTITUTIONS AND SERVICES

FEDERAL INTERVENTIONS IN RESPONSE TO THE FINANCIAL CRISIS

A RETROSPECTIVE OF COSTS

ALYSSA G. HARRINGTON
EDITOR

NOVINKA

New York

NOTICE TO THE READER

Library of Congress Cataloging-in-Publication Data

ISBN: 978-1-63485-347-7

Published by Nova Science Publishers, Inc. † New York

CONTENTS

PREFACE

In August 2007, asset-backed securities (ABS), particularly those backed by subprime mortgages, suddenly became illiquid and fell sharply in value as an unprecedented housing boom turned into a housing bust. Losses on the many ABS held by financial firms depleted their capital. Uncertainty about future losses on illiquid and complex assets led to firms having reduced access to private liquidity, sometimes catastrophically. In September 2008, the financial crisis reached panic proportions, with some large financial firms failing or having the government step in to prevent their failure. Initially, the government approach was largely ad hoc, addressing the problems at individual institutions on a case-by-case basis. The panic in September 2008 convinced policy makers that a system-wide approach was needed, and Congress created the Troubled Asset Relief Program (TARP) in October 2008. In addition to TARP, the Treasury, Federal Reserve (Fed) and Federal Deposit Insurance Corporation (FDIC) implemented broad lending and guarantee programs. The primary goal of the various interventions was to end the financial panic and restore normalcy to financial markets, rather than to make a profit for taxpayers. This book presents how much the programs ultimately cost (or benefited) the taxpayers based on straightforward cash accounting as reported by the various agencies. This book describes the various actions by the Federal Reserve to stabilize the financial markets and how those actions are likely to affect the federal budget in coming years. The book also presents estimates of the risk-adjusted (or fair-value) subsidies that the Federal Reserve provided to financial institutions through its emergency programs.

In: Federal Interventions in Response ... ISBN: 978-1-63485-347-7
Editor: Alyssa G. Harrington

Chapter 1

COSTS OF GOVERNMENT INTERVENTIONS IN RESPONSE TO THE FINANCIAL CRISIS: A RETROSPECTIVE*

Baird Webel and Marc Labonte

SUMMARY

In August 2007, asset-backed securities (ABS), particularly those backed by subprime mortgages, suddenly became illiquid and fell sharply in value as an unprecedented housing boom turned into a housing bust. Losses on the many ABS held by financial firms depleted their capital. Uncertainty about future losses on illiquid and complex assets led to firms having reduced access to private liquidity, sometimes catastrophically. In September 2008, the financial crisis reached panic proportions, with some large financial firms failing or having the government step in to prevent their failure.

Initially, the government approach was largely ad hoc, addressing the problems at individual institutions on a case-by-case basis. The panic in September 2008 convinced policy makers that a system-wide approach was needed, and Congress created the Troubled Asset Relief Program (TARP) in October 2008. In addition to TARP, the Treasury, Federal Reserve (Fed) and

* This is an edited, reformatted and augmented version of a Congressional Research Service publication R43413, prepared for Members and Committees of Congress dated February 27, 2014.

Federal Deposit Insurance Corporation (FDIC) implemented broad lending and guarantee programs. Because the crisis had many causes and symptoms, the response tackled a number of disparate problems and can be broadly categorized into programs that (1) increased financial institutions' liquidity; (2) provided capital directly to financial institutions for them to recover from asset write-offs; (3) purchased illiquid assets from financial institutions to restore confidence in their balance sheets and thereby their continued solvency; (4) intervened in specific financial markets that had ceased to function smoothly; and (5) used public funds to prevent the failure of troubled institutions that were deemed systemically important, popularly referred to as "too big to fail."

The primary goal of the various interventions was to end the financial panic and restore normalcy to financial markets, rather than to make a profit for taxpayers. In this sense, the programs were arguably a success. Nevertheless, an important part of evaluating the government's performance is whether financial normalcy was restored at a minimum cost to taxpayers. By this measure, the financial performance of these interventions far exceeded initial expectations that direct losses to taxpayers would run into the hundreds of billions of dollars.

Initial government outlays are a poor indicator of taxpayer exposure, because outlays were used to acquire or guarantee income-earning debt or equity instruments that could eventually be repaid or sold, potentially at a profit. For broadly available facilities accessed by financially sound institutions, the risk of default became relatively minor once financial markets resumed normal functioning. Most of the programs that were introduced have been wound down or have shrunk to a fraction of their previous size. This report presents how much the programs ultimately cost (or benefited) the taxpayers based on straightforward cash accounting as reported by the various agencies. Of the 23 programs reviewed in this report, principal repayment and income exceed initial outlays in 17, principal repayment and income fell short of initial outlays in three, and it is too soon to tell for the remaining three. Of the three programs that lost money, two assisted automakers, not financial firms. Altogether to date, realized gains across the various programs exceed realized losses by tens of billions of dollars. Most of the remaining principal outstanding is to Fannie Mae and Freddie Mac, where net income will exceed principal outstanding once recently announced quarterly payments are transferred. More sophisticated estimates that would take into account the complete economic costs of assistance, such as the time value of the funds involved, are not consistently available. In this sense, cash flow measures overestimate gains to the taxpayers.

INTRODUCTION

In August 2007, asset-backed securities (ABS), particularly those backed by subprime mortgages, suddenly became illiquid and fell sharply in value as an unprecedented housing boom turned into a housing bust. Losses on the many ABS held by financial firms depleted their capital. Uncertainty about future losses on illiquid and complex assets led to firms having reduced access to private liquidity, sometimes catastrophically.

In September 2008, the crisis reached panic proportions. Fannie Mae and Freddie Mac, government-sponsored enterprises (GSEs) who supported a large proportion of the mortgage market, were taken into government conservatorship. Lehman Brothers, a major investment bank, declared bankruptcy. The government acquired most of the equity in American International Group (AIG), one of the world's largest insurers, in exchange for an emergency loan from the Federal Reserve (Fed). These firms were seen by many, either at the time or in hindsight, as "too big to fail" firms whose failure would lead to contagion that would cause financial problems for counterparties or would disrupt the smooth functioning of markets in which the firms operated. One example of such contagion was the failure of a large money market fund holding Lehman Brothers debt that caused a run on many similar funds, including several whose assets were sound.

The federal government took a number of extraordinary steps to address widespread disruption to the functioning of financial markets. Initially, the government approach was largely an ad hoc one, attempting to address the problems at individual institutions on a case-by-case basis. The panic in September 2008 convinced policy makers that a larger and more systemic approach was needed, and Congress enacted the Emergency Economic Stabilization Act (EESA)[1] to create the Troubled Asset Relief Program (TARP) in October 2008. In addition to TARP, the Federal Reserve and Federal Deposit Insurance Corporation (FDIC) implemented broad lending and guaranty programs. Because the crisis had so many causes and symptoms, the response tackled a number of disparate problems, and can be broadly categorized into programs that

- increased institutions' liquidity (access to cash and easily tradable assets), such as direct lending facilities by the Federal Reserve or the FDIC's Temporary Liquidity Guarantee Program (TLGP);
- provided financial institutions with equity to rebuild their capital following asset write-downs, such as the Capital Purchase Program (CPP);
- purchased illiquid assets from financial institutions in order to restore confidence in their balance sheets in the eyes of investors, creditors, and counterparties, such as the Public-Private Partnership Investment Program (PPIP);
- intervened in specific financial markets that had ceased to function smoothly, such as the Commercial Paper Funding Facility (CPFF) and the Term Asset- Backed Securities Lending Facility (TALF);
- used public funds to prevent the failure of troubled institutions that were deemed by some "too big to fail" (TBTF) because of their systemic importance, such as AIG, Fannie Mae, and Freddie Mac.[2]

One possible schematic for categorizing the programs discussed in this report into these categories is presented in **Table 1**.

Although many arguments could be made for one particular form of intervention or another, the position could also be taken that the form of government support was not particularly important as long as it was done quickly and forcefully because what the financial system lacked in October 2008 was confidence, and any of several options might have restored confidence if it were credible. Some critics dispute that view, arguing that the panic eventually would have ended without government intervention, and that some specific government missteps exacerbated the panic.[3]

By 2010, many of the programs that were introduced had either expired or were shrinking. While funds could hypothetically still be outlayed under some programs today, in practice no new funds have been outlayed in recent years, nor is it expected that they will be in the future. The final cost—or gain—is now known for the programs that have been wound down, and a fairly reliable estimate can be made of whether the few remaining programs with funds outstanding will ultimately yield losses or gains.

Table 1. Programs Introduced During the Financial Crisis (by purpose)

Program	Institution Liquidity	Capital Injection	Illiquid Asset Purchase/Guarantee	Market Liquidity	TBTF Assistance
Treasury					
CPPa		X			X
US Automakers[a]	X	X			X
PPIP[a]			X		
MMMF Guarantee				X	
Federal Reserve					
TAF	X				
TSLF	X				
PDCF	X				
TALF[a]			X	X	
CPFF/AMLF	X			X	
Bear Stearns			X		X
Liquidity Swaps	X				
FDIC					
TLGP	X				
Joint Programs					
AIG[a]	X	X			X
GSEs	X	X		X	X
Citigroup[a]		X	X		X
Bank of America[a]		X	X		X

Source: The Congressional Research Service (CRS).

Note: See text below for formal names and details of these programs.

a. Program using TARP funds.

Congress has oversight responsibilities for the government's crisis response, through existing oversight committees and newly created entities such as a Special Inspector General for the TARP (SIGTARP), a Congressional Oversight Panel,[4] and a Financial Crisis Inquiry Commission. Congress is also interested in an accurate accounting of the costs of the crisis in the interest of determining how to cover the government's long-run costs. For example, Section 134 of EESA requires the President to propose a method for recouping TARP costs. On January 14, 2010, President Obama proposed a "Financial Crisis Responsibility Fee" to be levied on the debt of certain large financial firms to cover the costs of TARP. His proposal has not been enacted.

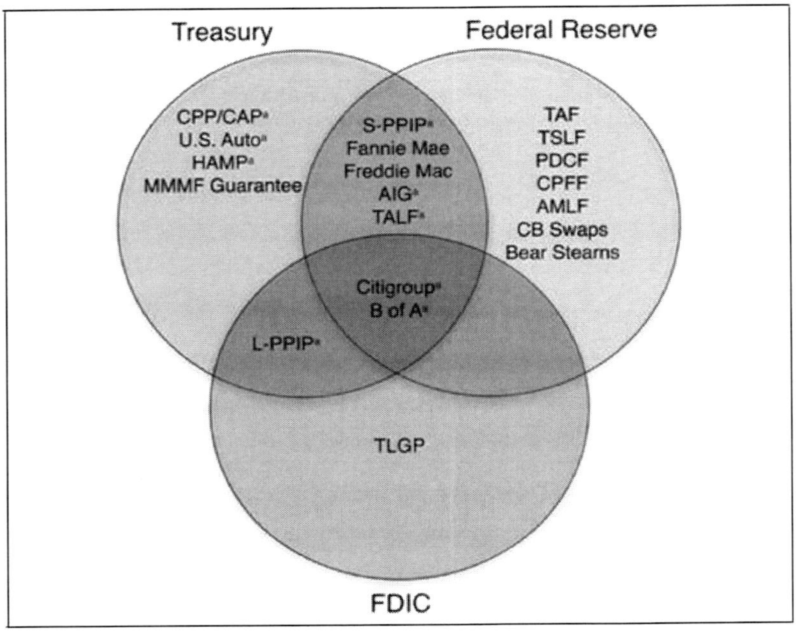

Source: CRS.
Notes: See text below for details of these programs.
a. Program using TARP funds.

Figure 1. Financial Crisis Programs by Organization.

This report reviews the costs of new programs introduced, and other actions taken, by the Treasury, Federal Reserve, and Federal Deposit Insurance Corporation.[5] **Figure 1** presents the programs discussed in this report by organization, with programs in the overlapping circles denoting joint programs. It does not cover long-standing programs, such as the Federal Reserve's discount window, mortgages guaranteed and securitized by the Federal Housing Administration and Ginnie Mae, respectively, or FDIC deposit insurance and receivership of failed banks.

Estimating the Costs of Government Interventions

The primary goal of the various interventions was to end financial panic and restore normalcy to financial markets. In this sense, the programs were arguably a success—based on traditional measures of market turbulence, such as the "TED Spread" (the difference between the 3-month LIBOR [London Interbank Offer Rate] and the 3-month Treasury rates), overall financial conditions significantly improved in late 2008 and returned to pre-crisis levels by mid-2009, although some specific markets took longer to rebound. The goal of intervening at zero cost to the taxpayers was never the best measure of success because non-intervention would likely have led to a much more costly loss of economic output that indirectly would have worsened the government's finances.[6] Further, the goal of maximizing return (or minimizing risk) to the government could work at odds with other policy goals, such as restoring investor confidence in the programs' recipients and encouraging voluntary participation in the government programs. Nevertheless, an important part of evaluating the government's actions is evaluating whether financial normalcy was restored at a minimum cost to the taxpayers.

One can distinguish in the abstract between funds provided to solvent companies and those provided to insolvent companies. For insolvent firms with negative net worth at the time of intervention, the government's chances of fully recouping losses are low.[7] For solvent firms, if properly implemented, it should be possible, in principle, to provide funds at a low ultimate cost, or even profit, to the taxpayers. In a panic, investors typically refuse to provide funds to firms because they are unable to distinguish between healthy and unhealthy firms, and so they err on the side of caution. For those private investors who perceive profitable opportunities to lend or invest, not enough liquidity may be available to do so. In this situation, the government can theoretically provide those funds to healthy firms at what would normally be a profitable market rate of return. In practice, the challenge is that the government is arguably no more able to accurately distinguish between healthy firms and unhealthy firms than private individuals are, so some widely available lending facilities are likely to be accessed by firms that will ultimately prove to be insolvent, and this is a possible source of long-term cost for a widely available facility.

At different times, news sources put the "potential cost to taxpayers," "amount taxpayers are on the hook for," and "taxpayer exposure" as a result of the financial crisis as high as $23.7 trillion.[8] These totals are reached by calculating the maximum potential size of programs or using the total size of markets being assisted when the programs have no announced potential size, and ignoring that at least some of the money that the government outlayed would eventually be paid back. Even official estimates that accounted for expected future repayment initially projected large losses. For example, in

March 2009, CBO projected that the government would ultimately pay a subsidy of $356 billion on TARP funds.[9]

Table 2. Programs Where Principal Repayments and Income Already Exceed Remaining Outlays

	Net Income	Principal Outstanding
Treasury		
Capital Purchase Program	$22.1 billion	$2.1 billion
PPIP-Legacy Securities	$3.9 billion	$0
Section 7(a) Securities	$0.01 billion	$0
Money Market Fund Guarantee	$1.2 billion	$0
Chrysler Financial	$0.01 billion	$0
GSE Senior Preferred Stock	$202.8 billion	$187.5 billion
Federal Reserve		
Term Auction Facility	$4.1 billion	$0
Term Securities Lending Facility	$0.8 billion	$0
Primary Dealer Credit Facility	$0.6 billion	$0
Asset-Backed Commercial Paper Money Market Liquidity Facility	$0.5 billion	$0
Commercial Paper Funding Facility	$6.1 billion	$0
Maiden Lane I	$0.8 billion	$0
FDIC		
Temporary Liquidity Guarantee Program (Debt Guarantee)	$10.2 billion	$0
Joint		
Term Asset-Backed Loan Facility	$2.1 billion	$0.1 billion
AIG (all programs)	$22.7 billion	$0
Citigroup (TIP and AGP)	$6.6 billion	$0
Bank of America (TIP and AGP)	$3.1 billion	$0

Source: See report tables below for sources and descriptions.

Notes: Net Income equals principal repayment plus dividend or interest income plus realized capital gains minus principal minus realized capital losses. CPP income from Citigroup and Bank of America is included in the CPP total only. All amounts are as of January 31, 2014, except Net Income for Term Asset-Backed Loan Facility and Maiden Lane I is as of September 30, 2013, and principal outstanding for TALF is as of October 31, 2013; Net income for the GSEs includes the quarterly payments announced on February 21 and 27, 2014, that are scheduled to be transferred to the U.S. Treasury in March 2014. Maiden Lane I held assets with a market value of $1.6 billion as of December 31, 2013; proceeds from the eventual sale or maturity of these assets will accrue to the Fed.

Actual financial results were quite different from these early estimates because, unlike typical government programs, outlays were mostly paid back in full with interest.[10] Altogether, the financial crisis programs covered in this report brought back more in principal repayments and income than was paid out. At this time, the vast majority of individual programs, including all Federal Reserve facilities, have already taken in more money than was paid out by the government (see **Table 2**). Even in those programs where losses were realized on specific transactions, such as the Capital Purchase Program, income from other transactions was more than sufficient to absorb those losses and still produce a net gain for the government. Programs in **Table 2** include both broadly based liquidity programs that could conceptually be structured to minimize the potential for losses, such as Fed lending facilities, and direct assistance to troubled companies, such as AIG, that were until recently thought likely to generate losses.

Six programs still have assistance outstanding. Of those six programs, three (GSE preferred shares, CPP, and TALF) have already generated net income in excess of remaining principal outstanding (see **Table 2**).[11] In other words, even if the value of all outstanding principal were written down to zero, these programs would still generate positive net income to the government. Of the other three programs (see **Table 3**), the Fed's purchases of GSE debt and TARP's assistance to Ally Financial are likely to ultimately generate positive net income for the government, but have not done so to date.[12] The Fed's GSE debt purchases could only generate losses for the government if the government withdrew its support from the GSEs and the GSEs defaulted on their debt—a scenario that is currently considered highly improbable, as evidenced by their low market yield. Two of the six programs (GSE preferred shares and Ally Financial shares) were until recently thought likely to generate losses. For example, through the first quarter of 2013, the GSE preferred shares had only generated $65.2 billion in dividends; in the four quarters since then, the shares have generated an additional $137.6 billion in income to the government, and net income now exceeds principal outstanding by $15 billion.

Table 3. Programs Where It is Unknown Whether Principal Repayments and Income Will Exceed Peak Outlays

	Net Income	Principal Outstanding
Treasury		
GMAC/Ally Financial	$4.6 billion	$5.7 billion
Community Development Capital Initiative	$0.03 billion	$0.47 billion
Fed		
GSE Debt Purchases (Fed)	$12.9 billion	$57.2 billion

Source: See report tables below for sources and descriptions.

Notes: Net Income equals principal repayment plus dividend or interest income plus capital gains minus principal minus realized capital losses. GSE data are for December 31, 2013, except net income on GSE Debt Purchases, which is September 30, 2013. Other data are for January 31, 2014.

Three programs realized net losses when assistance was exhausted (see **Table 4**). Note that while two of those recipients (GM and Chrysler) were victims of the financial crisis and received funding through emergency financial programs, they were not financial institutions. Thus, when limited to programs to aid the financial sector, only one program has realized losses for the government, whereas 16 have realized gains. Altogether to date, realized gains across the various programs exceed realized losses by tens of billions of dollars.

Table 4. Programs Where Net Losses Are Realized as of January 31, 2014

	Net Income	Principal Outstanding
Treasury		
GM	-$10.4 billion	$0
Chrysler	-$1.3 billion	$0
FDIC		
Transaction Account Guarantee	-$0.9 billion	$0

Source: See report tables below for sources and descriptions.

Notes: Net Income equals principal repayment plus dividend or interest income plus capital gains minus principal minus realized capital losses. Income for auto suppliers and warranty program are included in GM and Chrysler totals. Totals for TAG program do not include program of same name created by the Dodd-Frank Act.

Note that generating positive net income does not necessarily mean that these programs made an economic profit for the government. The government had to borrow, incurring interest payments, to finance these programs. For this reason, $1 lent out in 2008 was worth more than $1 repaid today, which **Tables 1, 2, and 3** do not account for. The government also faced significant risks at the time that money would not be fully repaid, even if it turned out after the fact that money was repaid. An economist would determine whether government programs were profitable by comparing the government's terms to what a private investor would require for the same investment. Making these adjustments would reduce the gains to the taxpayer shown in **Table 1**, and could even show losses on certain programs—although it is fair to question what terms should be used for a hypothetical private investor in the depths of the financial crisis, when private credit markets were not functioning.[13] In any case, if such a standard were used, it would be a more demanding one than the government typically uses to measure the costs of federal credit and guarantee programs.[14] The Congressional Budget Office (CBO), which adjusts for borrowing costs and risk, estimated in May 2013 that TARP would generate a subsidy of $5 billion in total.[15] There are no up-to-date official estimates for the other programs covered by this report.

Another long-term, and more amorphous, cost may be an increased likelihood of future rescues due to increased private-sector risk-taking brought on by the expectation that the government will provide a rescue again. In economic terms, this is referred to as "moral hazard," and the problem is particularly acute when assistance is provided to insolvent firms, at below market rates, or on similar terms to both risky and prudent firms.

For each program below, the Congressional Research Service (CRS) reports the latest data on government holdings or guarantees of assets or loans; the peak amount for the same measure; income earnings of the program from dividends, interest, or fees; estimates of the program's profits or losses; the dividend or interest rate charged by the program; warrants received in the transactions; subsequent modifications to the assistance (if any); and the expiration date for the program.

TROUBLED ASSET RELIEF PROGRAM

Treasury reacted quickly after the enactment of EESA, announcing the TARP Capital Purchase Program on October 14, 2008; several other programs followed. Listed below are the programs that were run primarily under TARP.

- **Capital Purchase Program (CPP).** Unlike the plan envisioned in the TARP legislative debate, the CPP did not purchase the mortgage-backed securities that were seen as toxic to the system, but instead purchased preferred shares in banks.[16] The resulting addition of capital, it was hoped, would allow banks to overcome the effect of the toxic assets while the assets remained on bank balance sheets. The CPP is now closed with no additional disbursements possible under the current program. Of the approximately $205 billion disbursed, $2.1 billion remains outstanding, $4.7 billion has been written off or recognized as a loss, and $26.8 billion in income has been received.[17]
- **Community Development Capital Initiative (CDCI).** The CDCI provided for lower dividend rates on preferred share purchases from banks that target their lending to low-income, underserved communities and small businesses. Many of the participants in the CDCI converted into the program from the CPP. This program is closed, with no additional disbursements possible under the current program. Of the $0.57 billion disbursed, $0.47 billion is still outstanding, $0.01 billion has been written off or recognized as a loss, and $0.04 in income has been received.
- **Public-Private Investment Program (PPIP).** This program provided funds and guarantees for purchases of mortgage-related securities from bank balance sheets. Purchases and management of the securities were done by private investors who have provided capital to invest along with the TARP funds. All of the $18.6 billion in disbursed PPIP funds have been repaid with $3.85 billion in income received and no realized losses.
- **Section 7(a) Securities Purchase Program.** This program supported the Small Business Administration's (SBA's) Section 7(a) loan program through purchases of pooled SBA guaranteed securities to increase credit availability for small businesses. It is now closed with $0.36 billion repaid out of the $0.37 billion in disbursed funds and $0.01 billion in income received.
- **Automobile Industry Support.**[18] This program initially provided loans to support General Motors (GM) and Chrysler and later included preferred share purchases from the auto financing company GMAC (now renamed Ally Financial) and a loan for Chrysler

Financial. The program ultimately resulted in majority government ownership of GM (60.8%) and GMAC/Ally Financial (74%), and minority government ownership of Chrysler (9.9%).

The U.S. government's ownership stake in GM was sold to GM itself and to the public between December 2010 and December 2013. The ownership stake in Chrysler was sold to Fiat in May 2011. A private share placement in January 2014 reduced the government's share of Ally Financial to 37%. The current total outstanding support to the auto industry is $5.7 billion of the $79.7 billion in disbursed funds, with $14.9 billion in recognized losses and $7.1 billion in income received. No new disbursements are possible under the current program.

- **Housing Assistance Programs.** These programs are unlike the other TARP programs in that they do not result in valuable assets or income in return for the TARP funding and thus will not be a focus of this report. A total of $10.9 billion has been disbursed out of $38.5 billion obligated.[19]

In some cases, the TARP programs were closely integrated with other agencies' assistance programs. Those programs are listed below under "Joint Interventions."

As of January 31, 2014, Treasury reported obligations under TARP totaling $456.6 billion authorized, with $422.6 billion disbursed. Of that total, $370.4 billion of funds paid out have already been returned to the Treasury and $33.1 billion have been written off or recognized as lost.[20] TARP was originally authorized to outlay up to $700 billion, however, this amount was reduced by Congress in July 2010.[21] Authorization to take on new commitments under TARP expired on October 3, 2010, however, outlays may continue under existing commitments and Treasury has indefinite authority to continue to hold and manage assets acquired under TARP.

Programs consisting solely of TARP funds are discussed immediately below, while those involving other agencies, such as the Federal Reserve and FDIC, are discussed under the heading "Joint Interventions."

Table 5.Troubled Asset Relief Program Funds

As of January 31, 2014	
Authorized	$475 billion[a]
Obligated	$456.6 billion
Disbursed	$422.6 billion
Returned	$370.4 billion
Written Off/Recognized Losses	$33.1 billion
Housing Funds Spent	$10.9 billion
Outstanding Funds	$8.2 billion
Income	$47.9 billion

Source: January 31, 2014, Daily TARP Update.

a. Original authorization was $700 billion, subsequently reduced by P.L. 111-22 and P.L. 111-203.

Capital Purchase Program and Capital Assistance Program

Under the Capital Purchase Program (CPP), $125 billion in capital was immediately provided to the nine largest banks (which became eight after a merger), with up to another $125 billion reserved for smaller banks that might wish to apply for funds through their primary federal banking regulator. This capital was provided in the form of preferred share purchases by TARP under contracts between the Treasury and banks. The initial contracts with the largest banks prevented these banks from exiting the program for three years. The contracts included dividend payments to be made on the preferred shares outstanding and the granting of warrants to the government that give it the option of acquiring the banks' common stock at a future date. By the end of 2008, the CPP had 214 participating banks with approximately $172.5 billion in share purchases outstanding.

The Obama Administration and the 111th Congress implemented changes to the CPP. EESA was amended, placing additional restrictions on participating banks in the existing CPP contracts, but also allowing for early repayment and withdrawal from the program without financial penalty.[22] With the advent of more stringent executive compensation restrictions for TARP recipients, many banks began to repay, or attempt to repay, TARP funds.

According to Treasury reports, by June 30, 2009, $70.1 billion of $203.2 billion CPP funds had been repaid; by December 31, 2009, $121.9 billion of $204.9 billion had been repaid; and by December 31, 2010, $167.93 billion of $204.9 billion had been repaid.

The new Administration also announced a review of the banking system, in which the largest participants were subject to stress tests to assess the adequacy of their capital levels. Satisfactory performance in the stress test was one regulatory requirement for large firms that wished to repay TARP funds. Large firms that appeared too fragile in the stress test would be required to raise additional capital, and the firms would have the option of raising that capital privately or from the government through a new Capital Assistance Program using TARP funds. No funding was provided through the Capital Assistance Program, although GMAC, formerly General Motors' financing arm, received funding to meet stress test requirements through the Automotive Industry Financing Program (discussed below). In addition, Citigroup, one of the initial eight large banks receiving TARP funds, agreed with the government to convert its TARP preferred shares into common equity to meet stress test requirements (see discussion of Citigroup below).

Beginning in 2012, Treasury began selling off some of its remaining CPP shares to the public through auctions to expedite the wind down of the program. In most cases, shares were sold at a discount to face value, resulting in a realized loss for TARP. Depending on each bank's financial condition and prospects, this outcome may or may not maximize the return to the taxpayer compared with continued government investment, but it contributes to the separate policy goal of minimizing the government's intervention in financial markets during normal conditions.

Treasury has not generally exercised warrants to take common stock in CPP recipients. Following the contracts initially agreed upon, Treasury has allowed institutions to purchase their warrants directly upon repayment of preferred shares, as long as both sides can reach an acceptable price. To reach an initial offering price, Treasury is using complex option pricing models to price the warrants that require assumptions to be made about future prices and interest rates. Because these pricing models are by their nature uncertain, some critics urge Treasury to auction the warrants on the open market (allowing the issuing firm to bid as well) to ensure that Treasury receives a fair price for them. Open auctions have been used, but only when an agreement between the Treasury and the firms cannot be reached.

CPP investments also earn income from dividends with a rate of 5% for the first five years and 9% thereafter. (For S-Corp banks, the dividend rate is 7.7% for the first five years and 13.8% thereafter.) Because most of the preferred shares were purchased in late 2008 or 2009, the increase in dividend rates has either already occurred or will occur shortly for most outstanding shares.

CPP profits stem from dividend payments and warrants received from recipients, and capital gains in limited cases when shares are sold for more than face value (typically, when banks exit TARP, they repurchase CPP shares at par value). Losses stem from the institution's failure, restructuring of the investment in an attempt to avoid failure, or sales of CPP shares to the public at less than par value. The ultimate profitability of the program will be determined by the balance between the two.

Table 6. Capital Purchase Program (as of January 31, 2014)

U.S. Treasury				**Terms and Conditions**		
Latest Asset Holdings	**Asset Holdings at Peak**	**Total Income**	**Realized Losses (-)**	**Dividend Rate**	**Warrants**	**Expiration Date**
$2.1 billion	$198.8 billion (March 2009)	$26.8 billion	-$4.7 billion	5% for first 5 years, 9% thereafter[a]	15% of preferred shares (5% immediately exercised for privately held banks)	Preferred Shares outstanding until repaid. No new contracts/ modifications after Oct. 3, 2010.

Source: January 31, 2014, Daily TARP Update; December 2013 TARP 105(a) Report; CBO, *Report on the Troubled Asset Relief Program—May 2013*; Various TARP Transactions Reports.

Notes: Data include preferred shares to Citigroup and Bank of America under CPP, which are also detailed in sections on assistance to those companies below. The amount disbursed, approximately $205 billion, is greater than the $198.8 billion of peak asset holdings because some repayments occurred prior to disbursement of the full amount.

a. For S-Corp banks, the dividend rate is 7.7% for the first five years and 13.8% thereafter.

Realized losses to date on the CPP preferred shares have been relatively small. As of January 31, 2014, Treasury reported $4.7 billion in write-offs and realized losses from the CPP. The largest portion of this amount was due to the failure of CIT Group, which had $2.3 billion in TARP shares outstanding when it failed. According to SIGTARP, of the 707 banks that received CPP funds, "Treasury sold its investments in 25 banks for less than par and its investments in 162 banks at auction (151 of those investments sold at a loss), and 28 institutions or their subsidiary banks failed, meaning Treasury lost its entire investment in those banks."[23]

More losses may be realized in the future, however. Of the 86 institutions remaining in TARP as of December 31, 2013, 61 had already missed dividend payments, according to SIGTARP.[24] Since there is no penalty for missed dividend payments and the dividend rate was moderate in the first five years, missed dividend payments are not necessarily a sign of weakness, but many of the CPP investments in which Treasury has already realized losses had previously missed dividend payments.[25]

The banks remaining in TARP are all small, so the government's remaining holdings of CPP shares ($2.1 billion as of January 31, 2014) are only a small fraction of its original holdings. To date, income in the form of dividend payments, capital gains, and warrant proceeds ($26.8 billion) has exceeded losses ($4.7 billion), to the extent that even if the value of all remaining outstanding funds were written down to zero, the program would yield positive cash flow on net. Of the $26.8 billion in total income, $6.9 billion comes from Citigroup alone (see the "Citigroup" section below). **Table 6** summarizes the CPP, including current and peak asset holdings, losses or gains, and conditions of the program.

Table 7. Community Development Capital Initiative (as of January 31, 2014)

U.S. Treasury				Terms and Conditions		
Latest Asset Holdings	Asset Holdings at Peak	Total Income	Realized Losses(-)	Interest/ Dividend Rate	Warrants	Expiration Date
$0.47 billion	$0.57 billion (Sept. 2012)	$0.04 billion	-$0.01 billion	2% (9% after 8 years)	none	No new purchases after Oct. 2010.

Source: January 31, 2014, TARP Daily Update; December 2013 TARP 105(a) Report.

Note: Of the disbursed funds, $210 million are new shares and $360 million are shares transferred from CPP.

Community Development Capital Initiative

The Community Development Capital Initiative (CDCI) operated somewhat like the CPP in that it purchased preferred shares from financial institutions; in some cases, institutions were permitted to convert previous CPP preferred shares to CDCI preferred shares. The program was specifically focused on institutions that serve low-income, underserved communities and small businesses. Treasury purchased preferred shares from institutions that qualified for the CDCI up to an amount equal to 5% of the institutions' risk-weighted assets for banks and thrifts or 3.5% of total assets for credit unions. These preferred shares pay an initial dividend rate of 2%, compared with 5% for the CPP, which will increase to 9% after eight years. Unlike the CPP, no warrants in the financial institutions were included. Purchases under the program were completed in September of 2010 with approximately $210 million in new shares purchased. In addition, approximately $360 million of shares were converted from CPP shares. Eighty-four banks and credit unions received funds, of which 28 had previously participated in CPP. Treasury has realized losses of $6.8 million on one failed institution. Two remaining participants have missed dividend payments.[26]

Public Private Investment Program

On March 23, 2009, Treasury announced the Public Private Investment Program (PPIP). PPIP as envisioned consisted of two asset purchase programs designed to leverage private funds with government funds to remove troubled assets from bank balance sheets. Perhaps closer to the original conception of TARP than other TARP programs, PPIP dedicated TARP resources as equity to (1) acquire troubled loans in a fund partially guaranteed by the FDIC and (2) acquire troubled securities in a fund designed to be used with loans from the Federal Reserve's TALF program or TARP. Both funds would match TARP money with private investment, and profits or losses would be shared between the government and the private investors. Unlike the original conception of TARP, private investors would choose the assets to purchase and manage the funds and the day-to-day disposition of assets. The legacy loan portion of PPIP never advanced past a single pilot sale reported by the FDIC on September 30, 2009.[27] Treasury originally envisioned asset purchases through PPIP would be as high as $1 trillion (using as much as $200 billion in

TARP funds), but a maximum of $22.4 billion was committed to the legacy securities portion of the program.

Legacy Securities Program

The PPIP Legacy Securities Program was designed to remove existing mortgage-related securities on bank balance sheets. Private investment fund managers applied to Treasury to pre-qualify to raise funds to participate in the program. Approved fund managers that raised private equity capital received matching Treasury capital and an additional loan to the fund that matched the private capital (thus, for example, a fund that raised $100 had a total of $300 available to invest). In addition to this basic transaction, Treasury had the discretion to allow another matching loan so that a fund raising $100 could have made a total of $400 available for investment. The funds were to be used to invest in non-agency MBS that originally received the highest credit rating (e.g., AAA). (Agency MBS refer to loans issued by GSEs, such as Fannie Mae and Freddie Mac, and non-agency MBS refers to mortgage-related securities issued by private financial institutions, such as investment banks.)

Nine funds were pre-qualified by the Treasury in June 2009. In early January 2010, however, one of the funds reached a liquidation agreement with Treasury and was wound down.[28] By March 31, 2013, another five of the funds had been effectively wound down and all $18.6 billion of the disbursed funds had been returned.[29] The program experienced no losses and earned income of $3.8 billion.

Table 8. Public Private Investment Program (as of January 31, 2014)

U.S. Treasury				Terms and Conditions			
Program	**Latest Asset Holdings/ Guaranteed**	**Asset Holdings/ Guaranteed at Peak**	**Total Income**	**Realized Losses(-)**	**Interest/ Dividend Rate**	**Warrants**	**Expiration Date**
Legacy Securities	$0	$16.1 billion (Nov. 2011)	$3.9 billion	None	LIBOR plus "applicable margin"	yes (amount unspecified)	10 years from creation of fund.

Sources: January 31, 2014, Daily TARP Update; November 2011 TARP 105(a) Report; U.S. Treasury, *Legacy Securities Public-Private Investment Program Update*, May 8, 2013; Congressional Oversight Panel, *Oversight Report*, September 2009; SIGTARP, *Quarterly Report to Congress*, January 30, 2010.

Section 7(a) Securities Purchase Program

This program supported the Small Business Administration's (SBA's) Section 7(a) loan program through purchases of pooled SBA guaranteed securities backed by private loans to small businesses.[30] Beginning in March 2010, Treasury purchased a total of $368 million in securities guaranteed by the SBA. Purchases ended in October 2010 with the expiration of the TARP authority and all securities have been sold or matured. Over the life of the program, income slightly exceeded lossses.

U.S. Automaker Assistance[31]

In addition to financial firms, non-financial firms also sought support under TARP, most notably U.S. automobile manufacturers.[32] EESA specifically authorized the Secretary of the Treasury to purchase troubled assets from "financial firms"; the legislative definition of this term did not mention manufacturing companies.[33] After separate legislation to provide federal funds to the automakers failed to clear Congress,[34] the Bush Administration turned to TARP for funding.

On December 19, 2008, the Bush Administration announced it was providing support through TARP to General Motors and Chrysler under the Automotive Industry Financing Program (AIFP). The initial package included up to $13.4 billion in a secured loan to GM and $4 billion in a secured loan to Chrysler. In addition, $884 million was lent to GM for its participation in a rights offering by GMAC as GM's former financing arm was becoming a bank holding company. On December 29, 2008, the Treasury announced that GMAC also was to receive a $5 billion capital injection through preferred share purchases.

After January 21, 2009, the Obama Administration continued assistance for the automakers, including support for the automaker warranties under the AIFP (so that consumers would not be discouraged from purchasing cars during the restructuring), and for third-party suppliers to the automakers (the Automotive Supplier Support Program). Additional loans for GM and Chrysler were made before and during the two companies' bankruptcies, and GMAC received additional capital through preferred share purchases as well. At the end of 2009, GM had received approximately $50.2 billion in direct loans and indirect support; Chrysler had received $10.9 billion in loans and indirect support; GMAC had received $17.2 billion in preferred equity purchases and indirect support; and Chrysler Financial had received $1.5 billion in loans.

Most of the assistance has been repaid or recognized as a loss by the Treasury. As of January 31, 2014, TARP support for the auto industry totaled approximately $79.7 billion disbursed, with $59.1 billion repaid and $7.1 billion in income. Approximately $14.9 billion has been written off or taken as a realized loss and $5.7 billion of assistance is outstanding. The only assistance outstanding takes the form of government ownership of 37% of the common equity in Ally Financial (formerly GMAC). Were the government to sell its remaining Ally Financial equity holdings at the same price it received for previous sales, the transaction would be cash-flow positive. Whether this is still true when the government sells its holdings will depend on market prices at that time.

FEDERAL RESERVE

Beginning in December 2007, the Federal Reserve introduced a number of emergency credit facilities to provide liquidity to various segments of the financial system.[35] Most, but not all, of these facilities make short-term loans backed by collateral that exceeds the value of the loan, with recourse to the borrower's other assets if the borrower defaults. These facilities were widely available to all qualified participants. (Fed assistance to individual companies is discussed separately below.) Since the Fed's creation 100 years ago, the Fed has always made short-term collateralized loans to banks through its discount window. In the years before the crisis, loans outstanding through the discount window were consistently less than $1 billion at any time. At the peak of the crisis, total assistance outstanding would peak at more than $1 trillion. Another attribute that distinguished these new facilities from the Fed's traditional lending was the fact that many served non-banks that were not regulated by the Fed.

Profits or losses on Fed lending accrue to the taxpayer similar to if the loans had been made by the Treasury. The Fed generates income from its assets and loans that exceed its expenses. Any income that remains after expenses, dividends, and additions to its surplus is remitted to the Treasury. If its profits rise because its lending facilities are more profitable than alternative uses, more funds will be remitted to the Treasury. If it suffers losses on its facilities, its remittances to the Treasury will fall. The risk to most of the Fed's broad credit facilities was relatively low since the loans are short-term, collateralized, and the Fed had the right to refuse borrowers it deemed to be not credit-worthy. (As discussed below, the Fed's assistance to firms deemed "too big to fail" was significantly riskier.) In 2009, the Fed remitted $46 billion to the Treasury. This was $11 billion more than 2007 and $14 billion more than in 2008. In that sense, taxpayers have profited from the creation of the Fed's lending facilities, although that was not their purpose and those facilities were not risk free.

The Fed has standing authority to lend to banks and buy certain assets, such as GSE-issued securities. For many new programs, the Fed relied on broad emergency authority (Section 13(3) of the Federal Reserve Act) that had not been used since the 1930s.[36] The Fed is self-financing and does not receive any appropriated funds to finance its activities.

Since early 2009, credit outstanding under most of these facilities has consistently fallen, primarily because financial firms have begun returning to private sources of funding as financial conditions have improved. Most emergency facilities expired on February 1, 2010, after multiple extensions, and most had no outstanding balance after that point. The Fed reported no losses and positive income on all of these facilities.

Table 9. Section 7(a) Securities Purchase Program (as of January 31, 2014)

Federal Government				Terms and Conditions			
Program	**Latest Asset Holdings**	**Asset Holdings at Peak**	**Total Income (Life of Program)**	**Realized Losses(-)**	**Interest/ Dividend Rate**	**Warrants**	**Expiration Date**
Section 7(a) Securities	$0	$367 million	$13 million	- $4 million	floating	none	No new purchases after Oct. 2010.

Sources: January 31, 2014, Daily TARP Update; September 2012 TARP 105(a) Report; SIG TARP Quarterly Report to Congress, April 25, 2012.

Table 10. Government Support to the Auto Industry (as of January 31, 2014)

Federal Government					Terms and Conditions		
Beneficiary/ Program	Latest Asset Holdings	Total Assistance at Peak	Total Income	Realized Losses(-)	Dividend/ Interest Rate	Subsequent Conversion	Expiration Date
GM	$0	$49.5 billion loans	$0.68 billion	-$11.2 billion	LIBOR + 5%	Loan converted into 60.8% of common equity and preferred stock.	January 2015 (loan for New GM); December 2011 (loan for Old GM)
GMAC/Ally Financial	$5.7 billion in common equity	$16.3 billion convertible preferred stock; $884 million loan through GM	$4.6 billion	-$0.9 billion	9%	Loan and preferred shares converted into 56.3% of common equity	No expiration
Chrysler	$0	$10.5 billion drawn of $14.9 billion loan commitments.	$1.6 billion	-$2.9 billion	LIBOR + 7.9%; LIBOR + 3%; LIBOR + 5%	Loans converted to 9.9% of common equity; $1.9 billion recouped in bankruptcy process	June 2017; January 2012
Chrysler Financial	$0	$1.5 billion loan	$7 million	$0		None	January 2014
Auto Suppliers	$0	$413 million drawn of $5.0 billion loan commitment	$116 million	$0	Greater of LIBOR+ 3.5% or 5.5%	None	April 2010
GM and Chrysler Warranty Commitment	$0	$641 million	$5.5 million	$0	LIBOR+3.5%	None	July 2009

Source: January 31, 2014, Daily TARP Update; TARP 105(a) Report, various dates; TARP Dividends and Interest Report, various dates; Congressional Oversight Panel September 2009 Oversight Report; CBO, *Report on the Troubled Asset Relief Program*, various dates; SIGTARP, *Quarterly Report to Congress*, September 30, 2010; U.S. Treasury Office of Financial Stability, *Agency Financial Report Fiscal Year 2010*, November 2010.

Estimating a subsidy rate on Fed lending is not straightforward, and some would argue is not meaningful. The Fed's loans are usually made at some modest markup above the federal funds rate; in that sense they can be considered higher than market rates—whether the markup is high enough to avoid a subsidy depends on the riskiness of the facility.[37] But the Fed controls the federal funds rate, even though it is a private market for overnight inter-bank lending. During the crisis, the Fed drove the federal funds rate gradually down from 5.25% in September 2007 to nearly zero in December 2008 by creating the liquidity needed to avert a crisis; as a result, its direct loans were made at a very low rate. Because the purpose of the Fed is to supply financial markets with adequate liquidity, which has some characteristics of what economists call a "public good" that cannot always be provided by the private sector, it is not clear that reducing the federal funds rate should be classified as a subsidy. Further, the Fed would argue that it was only providing credit because there was no private sector alternative during the crisis, and borrowing from the Fed fell relatively quickly in 2009 once financial conditions began to normalize.

The Fed reports extensive data on its activities. Outstanding balances for each facility are available on a weekly basis from the H.4.1 data release, *Factors Affecting Reserve Balances of Depository Institutions*. Detailed information on the number of borrowers, concentration of loans, types of collateral, and overall earnings for each facility is available on a monthly basis in *Federal Reserve System Monthly Report on Credit and Liquidity Programs and the Balance Sheet*. The Fed disclosed details of specific transactions, notably the identities of recipients and specific collateral posted, on December 1, 2010, as required by the Dodd-Frank Act (P.L. 111- 203).[38] In addition, oversight reports have been produced by the Government Accountability Office[39] and the Fed's Inspector General.[40]

Term Auction Facility

In December 2007, the Fed created its first facility in response to financial conditions, the Term Auction Facility (TAF). This facility auctioned reserves to banks in exchange for collateral. Economically and legally, this facility was equivalent to the discount window, and was created primarily out of a concern that banks were not accessing the discount window as much as needed as a result of the stigma associated with discount window lending. Since this facility was not created with emergency authority, it need not be temporary, but the Fed has held no auctions since March 8, 2010.

Any depository institution eligible for discount window lending could participate in the TAF, and hundreds at a time accessed the TAF and the discount window since its inception. The auction process determined the rate at which those funds were lent, with all bidders receiving the lowest winning bid rate. The winning bid could not be lower than the prevailing federal funds rate. Auctions through the TAF were held twice a month beginning in December 2007. The amounts auctioned greatly exceeded discount window lending, which averaged in the hundreds of millions of dollars outstanding daily before 2007 and more than $10 billion outstanding during the crisis. Loans outstanding under the facility peaked at $493 billion in March 2009, and fell steadily until reaching zero when the facility expired in March 2010. Between the discount window and the TAF, banks were consistently the largest private sector recipient of Fed assistance since 2007.

Risks to the Fed were limited by collateral requirements, the short duration of the loans, and recourse requirements. TAF loans matured in 28 days—far longer than overnight loans in the federal funds market or the typical discount window loan. (In July 2008, the Fed began making some TAF loans that matured in 84 days.) Like discount window lending, TAF loans must be fully collateralized with the same qualifying collateral accepted by the discount window. Loans previously made by depository institutions and asset-backed securities were the most frequently posted collateral. Although not all collateral has a credit rating, those that are rated typically had the highest rating. Most borrowers borrowed much less than the posted collateral. Over the life of the program, the Fed experienced no losses and earned income of $4.1 billion from the TAF.

Table 11. Term Auction Facility

Federal Reserve				**Terms and Conditions**	
Current Loans Outstanding	**Loans Outstanding at Peak**	**Total Income (Life of Program)**	**Realized Losses(-)**	**Lending Rate**	**Expiration Date**
$0	$493 billion in March 2009	$4.1 billion	$0	Set by auction; no lower than federal funds rate	March 8, 2010

Source: CRS Report RL34427, *Financial Turmoil: Federal Reserve Policy Responses*, by Marc Labonte.

Term Securities Lending Facility

Shortly before Bear Stearns suffered its liquidity crisis in March 2008, the Fed created the Term Securities Lending Facility (TSLF) to expand its securities lending program for primary dealers. Primary dealers are financial firms that the Fed conducts transactions with for purposes of open market operations and include investment banks that were ineligible to access the Fed's lending facilities for banks. The proximate cause of Bear Stearns' crisis was its inability to roll over its short-term debt, and the Fed created the TSLF and the Primary Dealer Credit Facility (discussed below) to offer an alternative source of short-term liquidity for primary dealers.

Under the TSLF at its peak, each week primary dealers could borrow up to $200 billion of Treasury securities for 28 days instead of overnight. Access to Treasury securities is important for primary dealers because of their use in repurchase agreements ("repos") that are an important source of short-term financing. Loans could be collateralized with private-label MBS with an AAA/Aaa rating, agency commercial mortgage-backed securities, and agency collateralized mortgage obligations.[41] On September 14, 2008, the Fed expanded acceptable collateral to include all investment-grade debt securities. No securities were borrowed through the TSLF after August 2009, and the facility expired February 1, 2010. It experienced no losses and earned income of $781 million over the life of the program.

Table 12. Term Securities Lending Facility

Federal Reserve				Terms and Conditions	
Current Loans Outstanding	**Loans Outstanding at Peak**	**Total Income (Life of Program)**	**Realized Losses (-)**	**Fee**	**Expiration Date**
$0	$235.5 billion on Oct. 1, 2008	$781 million	$0	Set at auction, with minimum fee of 10 to 25 basis points	Feb. 1, 2010

Source: Federal Reserve, Office of the Inspector General, *The Federal Reserve's Section 13(3) Lending Facilities to Support Overall Market Liquidity*, Nov. 2010.

Primary Dealer Credit Facility

Shortly after Bear Stearns' liquidity crisis, the Fed created the Primary Dealer Credit Facility (PDCF), which can be thought of as analogous to a discount window for primary dealers. Loans were made at the Fed's discount rate, which was set slightly higher than the federal funds rate during the crisis. Loans were made on an overnight basis, with recourse, and fully collateralized, limiting their riskiness. Acceptable collateral initially included Treasuries, government agency debt, and investment grade corporate, mortgage-backed, asset-backed, and municipal securities. On September 14, 2008, the Fed expanded acceptable collateral to include certain classes of equities. The Primary Dealer Credit Facility expired on February 1, 2010.

Borrowing from the facility was sporadic, with average daily borrowing outstanding above $10 billion in the first three months, and falling to zero in August 2008. Much of this initial borrowing was done by Bear Stearns, before its merger with J.P. Morgan Chase had been completed. Loans outstanding through the PDCF picked up again in September 2008 and peaked at $148 billion on October 1, 2008. After May 2009, outstanding loans through the PDCF were zero, presumably because the largest investment banks converted into or were acquired by bank holding companies in late 2008, making them eligible to access other Fed lending facilities. The PDCF experienced no losses and earned interest income of $0.5 billion over the life of the program.

Table 13. Primary Dealer Credit Facility

Federal Reserve				**Terms and Conditions**	
Current Loans Outstanding	**Loans Outstanding at Peak**	**Total Income (Life of Program)**	**Realized Losses(-)**	**Lending Rate/Fee**	**Expiration Date**
$0	$147 billion on Oct. 1, 2008	$0.6 billion	$0	Rate set equal to Fed's discount rate; fees of up to 40 basis points for frequent users	Feb. 1, 2010

Source: Federal Reserve, Office of the Inspector General, *The Federal Reserve's Section 13(3) Lending Facilities to Support Overall Market Liquidity*, November 2010.

Commercial Paper Funding Facility and Asset-Backed Commercial Paper Money Market Mutual Fund Liquidity Facility

To meet liquidity needs, many large firms routinely issue commercial paper, which is short-term debt purchased directly by investors that matures in less than 270 days, with an average maturity of 30 days. There are three broad categories of commercial paper issuers: financial firms, non- financial firms, and pass-through entities that issue commercial paper backed by assets. The commercial paper issued directly by firms tends not to be backed by collateral, as these firms are viewed as large and creditworthy, and the paper matures quickly.

Individual investors are major purchasers of commercial paper through money market mutual funds and money market accounts. A run on a money market fund on September 16, 2008, greatly decreased the demand for new commercial paper.[42] Firms rely on the ability to issue commercial paper to roll over maturing debt to meet their liquidity needs.

Fearing that disruption in the commercial paper markets could make overall problems in financial markets more severe, the Fed announced on September 19, 2008, that it would create the Asset- Backed Commercial Paper Money Market Mutual Fund Liquidity Facility (AMLF). This facility made non-recourse loans to banks to purchase asset-backed commercial paper. Because the loans were non-recourse, the banks had no further liability to repay any losses on the commercial paper collateralizing the loan. At its peak in early October 2008, there were daily loans of $152 billion outstanding through the AMLF. The AMLF would soon be superseded in importance by the creation of the Commercial Paper Funding Facility, and lending fell to zero in October 2009. It experienced no losses and earned income of $0.5 billion over the life of the program. The facility expired on February 1, 2010.

On October 7, 2008, the Fed announced the creation of the Commercial Paper Funding Facility (CPFF) to purchase all types of three-month, highly rated U.S. commercial paper, secured and unsecured, from issuers. The interest rate charged by the CPFF was set at the three month overnight index swap rate plus 1 percentage point for secured corporate debt, 2 percentage points for unsecured corporate debt, and 3 percentage points for asset-backed paper. The CPFF could buy as much commercial paper from any individual issuer as that issuer had outstanding in the year to date. Any potential losses borne by the CPFF would ultimately be borne by the Fed. At its peak in January 2009, the CPFF held $351 billion of commercial paper, and holdings fell steadily subsequently. The facility expired February 1, 2010. It earned income of $6.1 billion over the life of the program and suffered no losses.

In the case of the AMLF, the banks were not intended recipients of assistance, but rather were meant to be the intermediary through which assistance flowed to the commercial paper market. The CPFF essentially removed the role of banks as intermediary and provided Fed assistance directly to CP issuers.[43]

Table 14. Asset-Backed Commercial Paper Money Market Mutual Fund Liquidity Facility

Federal Reserve				Terms and Conditions	
Current Loans Outstanding	**Loans Outstanding at Peak**	**Total Income (Life of Program)**	**Realized Losses (-)**	**Lending Rate**	**Expiration Date**
$0	$152.1 billion on Oct. 1, 2008	$0.5 billion	$0	Fed's Discount Rate	Feb. 1, 2010

Source: Federal Reserve, Office of the Inspector General, The Federal Reserve's Section 13(3) Lending Facilities to Support Overall Market Liquidity, November 2010.

Table 15. Commercial Paper Funding Facility

Federal Reserve				Terms and Conditions	
Current Loans Outstanding	**Loans Outstanding at Peak**	**Total Income (Life of Program)**	**Realized Losses(-)**	**Interest Rate/Fees**	**Expiration Date**
$0	$348.2 billion on Jan. 21, 2009	$6.1 billion	$0	Markups of 100 to 300 basis points over overnight index swap rate; fees of 10 to 100 basis points	Feb. 1, 2010

Source: Federal Reserve, Office of the Inspector General, The Federal Reserve's Section 13(3) Lending Facilities to Support Overall Market Liquidity, November 2010.

On October 21, 2008, the Fed announced the creation of the Money Market Investor Funding Facility (MMIFF), and pledged to lend it up to $540 billion. The MMIFF was planned to lend to private sector special purpose vehicles (SPVs) that invest in commercial paper issued by highly rated financial institutions. Each SPV would have been owned by a group of financial firms and could only purchase commercial paper issued by that group. The intent was for these SPVs to purchase commercial paper from money market mutual funds and similar entities facing redemption requests to help avoid runs such as the run on the Reserve Fund. The MMIFF was never accessed, and the facility expired on October 30, 2009.

Bear Stearns

Unable to roll over its short-term debt as a result of investor concerns about its mortgage-related losses, the investment bank Bear Stearns faced bankruptcy. Fearing that Bear Stearns was "too big to fail" and posed systemic risk,[44] the Fed stepped in to broker a merger. On March 16, 2008, JPMorgan Chase agreed to acquire Bear Stearns. As part of the agreement, the Fed agreed to lend $28.82 billion to Maiden Lane I, a Delaware limited liability corporation (LLC) that it created, to purchase financial securities at current market value from Bear Stearns. These securities were largely mortgage-related assets that were too illiquid for JPMorgan Chase to be willing to acquire.

Table 16. Bear Stearns Support (Maiden Lane I, LLC)

Federal Reserve					Terms and Conditions	
Current Loans to Fed Outstanding	**Original Fed Loan Balance (June 26, 2008)**	**Net Value of Remaining Assets (Dec. 31, 2013)**	**Net Income to Fed (Sep. 30, 2013)**	**Realized Losses(-)**	**Interest Rate**	**Expiration Date**
$0 billion	$28.8 billion	$1.6 billion	$765 million	$0	discount rate	Securities held long term

Source: Federal Reserve Bank of New York, *Maiden Lane Transactions*, http://www.newyorkfed.org/markets/ maidenlane.html.

Interest and principal was to be repaid to the Fed by Maiden Lane I using the funds raised by the sale of the assets, not by JP Morgan Chase. JPMorgan Chase took a first loss position through a subordinated loan of $1.15 billion, and received an interest rate of 4.5% above the discount rate on that position, compared with an interest rate of 2.5% above the discount rate on the Fed's loan. Any additional losses would be borne by the Fed, and any profits in excess of the loans would accrue to the Fed. Profits or losses for the Fed and JPMorgan Chase were dependent on whether the market value of those assets rose or declined after Maiden Lane I acquired them.

By November 2012, proceeds from the sale or maturation of Maiden Lane I assets were sufficient to fully repay principal and accrued interest to the Fed ($765 million) and JPMorgan Chase. As of December 30, 2013, the value of remaining assets held by Maiden Lane I was $1.6 billion.[45] Once those remaining assets are sold or have matured, the Fed will realize capital gains that would be greater or less than $1.6 billion (less expenses), depending on whether the value of those assets subsequently rises or falls.

FEDERAL DEPOSIT INSURANCE CORPORATION

The FDIC has undertaken a significant role in the financial crisis through its standing authority to resolve failed banks and administer the federal guarantees on individual deposits (actions that are beyond the scope of this report). In addition, the FDIC has carried out several exceptional measures, including a broad guarantee program on debt issued by banks and supporting combined interventions in Citigroup and Bank of America (see "Joint Interventions").

Temporary Liquidity Guarantee Program

On October 14, 2008, the FDIC announced the creation of the Temporary Liquidity Guarantee Program (TLGP), consisting of a Debt Guarantee Program (DGP) and a Transaction Guarantee Program (TAG), to support liquidity and discourage runs in the banking system.[46] This program was not specifically authorized by Congress; it was authorized under the FDIC's standing systemic risk mitigation authority.[47] Financial institutions eligible for participation in the TLGP program included entities insured by the FDIC, bank holding and financial holding companies headquartered in the United States, and savings and loan companies under Section 4(k) of the Bank Holding Company Act.[48] Although the TLGP was a voluntary program, eligible financial institutions were automatically registered to participate unless they had opted out by November 12, 2008.[49]

The Debt Guarantee Program guaranteed bank debt, including commercial paper, interbank funding debt, promissory notes, and any unsecured portion of secured debt.[50] The program originally applied to debt issued before June 30, 2009, but was extended in March 2009 to apply to debt issued before October 31, 2009. The guarantee remained in effect until December 31, 2012. Fees for the guarantees were up to 1.1% of the guaranteed debt on an annualized basis with additional surcharges of up to 0.5%, depending on the maturity length of the debt and whether or not the institution is FDIC insured.[51]

Upon the expiration of the Debt Guarantee Program the FDIC established a limited successor program to "ensure an orderly phase-out" of the program.[52] This six-month emergency guarantee facility was limited to certain participating entities, who must apply to the FDIC for permission to issue FDIC-guaranteed debt during the period starting October 31, 2009, through April 30, 2010. The fee for issuing debt under the emergency facility was to be at least 3%. The FDIC has not separately reported any use of the emergency guarantee program.

The Transaction Account Guarantee insured all non-interest-bearing deposit accounts, extending FDIC insurance beyond the $250,000 deposit insurance limit. The accounts primarily benefiting from TAG were accounts used by businesses and local governments, such as payroll processing accounts. In June 2010, the FDIC extended the TAG portion of the TLGP through December 31, 2010.[53] For institutions that chose to remain in the program, the fee would range from 0.15% to 0.25% depending on the institution's risk.[54]

TAG was not further extended due to the provisions in the Dodd-Frank Act[55] which provided for full deposit insurance coverage for noninterest-bearing transaction accounts for two years, without opt outs or a specified funding source. (This program is also often popularly referred to as TAG, however.) The FDIC reported guaranteed deposits of $1.5 trillion, but did not report fees or losses, under this program.[56] Insurance coverage pursuant to the Dodd-Frank Act expired on December 31, 2012.[57]

Table 17. Temporary Liquidity Guarantee Program

FDIC					Terms and Conditions	
Program	Current Debt Guaranteed	Debt Guaranteed at Peak	Total Income	Realized Losses(-)	Fee	Expiration Date
Debt Guarantee	$0	$345.8 billion (May 31, 2009)	$10.4 billion	-$0.2 billion	0.5%-1.1% annualized rate plus up to 0.5% surcharge; at least 3% for emergency extension.	Guarantees debt issued before Oct. 31, 2009, until Dec. 31 2012; emergency extension for debt issued before Apr. 30, 2010.
Transaction Account Guarantee (FDIC initiated)	$0	$834 billion (Dec. 31, 2009)	$1.2 billion	-$2.1 billion	0.15% to 0.25%	Dec. 31, 20

Source: FDIC, *Temporary Liquidity Guarantee Program*, http:// www.fdic.gov/ regulations/resources/TLGP/ index.html; FDIC, *Temporary Liquidity Guarantee Program Frequently Asked Questions*, http://www.fdic.gov/regulations/ resources/TLGP/faq.html; FDIC, *Quarterly Banking Profile*, various dates.

Note: Data on the Transaction Account Guarantee Program does not include the Transaction Account Guarantee Program created by the Dodd-Frank Act.

Participation in the TGLP was widespread at its peak, with almost 90% of FDIC-insured institutions participating in TAG and more than half in DGP. At its peak, the DGP guaranteed $345.8 billion in debt and the TAG guaranteed $834 billion in deposits in 2009. Over its life, the TAG program collected $1.2 billion in fees, insufficient to cover $2.1 billion in losses. By contrast, the DGP collected $10.4 billion in fees, more than offsetting $0.2 billion in losses.[58]

U.S. Department of the Treasury

Prior to the passage of EESA and the implementation of TARP, the Treasury had comparatively little authority to intervene in financial markets. It did, however, implement one program intended to end the money market run.

Money Market Mutual Fund Guarantee Program

On September 16, 2008, a money market mutual fund called the Reserve Fund "broke the buck," meaning that the value of its shares had fallen below par value of $1. This occurred because of losses it had taken on short-term debt issued by Lehman Brothers, which filed for bankruptcy on September 15, 2008. Money market investors had perceived "breaking the buck" to be highly unlikely, and its occurrence set off a generalized run on money market funds, as investors simultaneously attempted to withdraw an estimated $250 billion of their investments—even from funds without exposure to Lehman.[59]

To stop the run, Treasury announced an optional program to guarantee deposits in participating money market funds. Treasury would finance any losses from this guarantee with assets in the Exchange Stabilization Fund (ESF), funds intended to protect the value of the dollar. Treasury announced this program without seeking specific congressional authorization, justifying the program on the grounds that guaranteeing money market funds would protect the value of the dollar. After the fact, Congress addressed the money market guarantee in Section 131 of EESA, reimbursing the ESF from EESA funds, but also forbidding the future use of the ESF to provide such a guarantee. The program expired after one year in September 2009. Over the life of the program, Treasury reported that no guaranteed funds had failed, and $1.2 billion in fees had been collected. More than $3 trillion of deposits were guaranteed and, according to the Bank for International Settlements, 98% of money market mutual funds were covered by the guarantee, with most exceptions being funds that invested only in Treasury securities.[60]

Depositors in the Reserve Fund were not covered by this program, but the ESF was used to purchase its $3.6 billion holdings of GSE securities in order to increase its liquidity.

Joint Interventions

Term Asset-Backed Securities Loan Facility

In November 2008, the Fed created the Term Asset-Backed Securities Loan Facility (TALF) in response to problems in the market for asset-backed securities (ABS). According to the Fed, "new issuance of ABS declined precipitously in September and came to a halt in October. At the same time, interest rate spreads on AAA-rated tranches of ABS soared to levels well outside the range of historical experience, reflecting unusually high risk premiums."[61] Data support the Fed's view: issuance of non-residential mortgage asset-backed securities fell from $902 billion in 2007 to $5 billion in the fourth quarter of 2008, according to the Securities Industry and Financial Markets Association. The Fed feared that if lenders could not securitize these types of loans, less credit would be extended to consumers, and eventually households would be forced to reduce consumption spending, exacerbating the economic downturn.

Rather than purchase ABS directly, the Fed made non-recourse loans to private investors to purchase recently issued ABS receiving the highest credit rating, using the ABS as collateral. The minimum loan size was $10 million. Eligible collateral included new securities backed by auto loans, student loans, small business loans, and credit card loans. TALF was later expanded to include "legacy" commercial mortgage-backed securities as part of the Public Private Investment Program discussed above. The loans have a term of up to three years for most types of assets (and up to five years for some types of assets). Interest rates were set at a markup over different maturities of the London inter-bank offered rate (LIBOR) or the federal funds rate, depending on the type of loan and underlying collateral.

If the ABS lose value, because the loans were non-recourse, the losses would be borne by the Fed and the Treasury (through TARP) instead of by the borrower—an unusual feature that makes TALF riskier for taxpayers than typical Fed lending facilities. The Fed lent less than the current value of the collateral, so the Fed would not bear losses on the loan until losses exceed the value of this reduction or "haircut" (different ABS receive different haircuts). In addition, Treasury initially set aside $20 billion of TARP funds to cover any losses.[62]

TALF turned out to be a relatively small program compared to the $200 billion program envisioned by the Fed or the $1 trillion program later envisioned by Treasury. In part, this was because the issuance of assets eligible for TALF has remained low, which reflected the continuing depressed state of securitization markets and may imply that TALF has been unable to overcome current investor aversion to ABS. (While TALF was in operation beginning in March 2009, a sizable share of ABS issued were used as collateral for TALF loans. Thus, issuance might have been even lower without the presence of TALF.)

Table 18. Money Market Mutual Fund Guarantee Program

Federal Government					Terms and Conditions	
Program	**Current Deposits Guaranteed/Assets**	**Deposits Guaranteed/ Assets Held at Peak**	**Total Income, Life of Program**	**Realized Losses(-)**	**Fee**	**Expiration Date**
MMMF Guarantee	$0	over $3 trillion (life of program)	$1.2 billion	$0	1.5% to 2.3% of shares guaranteed	Sept. 18, 2009
Purchase of Reserve Fund's Assets	n/a	$3.6 billion	n/a	n/a	n/a	n/a

Source: CBO, *Budget and Economic* Outlook, January 2009; U.S. Department of Treasury, press release, December 9, 2009; U.S. Department of Treasury, press release, September 29, 2008.

Table 19. Term Asset-Backed Securities Loan Facility

Federal Reserve			Terms and Conditions		
Current Loans Outstanding (Oct. 31, 2013)	**Loans Outstanding at Peak**	**Total Income**	**Realized Losses(-)**	**Lending Rate/Fee**	**Expiration Date**
$0.1 billion	$48.2 billion on Mar. 17, 2010	$1.6 billion to Fed as of Sept. 30, 2013; $0.6 billion to Treasury as of Jan. 31, 2014	$0	Various markups over LIBOR or federal funds rate; 10 to 20 basis point administrative fee	No new purchases after Mar. 31, 2010 (June 30, 2010, for new CMBS)

Source: Federal Reserve, Office of the Inspector General, The Federal Reserve's Section 13(3) Lending Facilities to Support Overall Market Liquidity, Nov. 2010; Federal Reserve, Combined Financial Statements, various dates; January 31, 2014, Daily TARP Update.

The facility stopped making new loans at the end of June 2010 for loans using newly issued CMBS as collateral and in March 2010 for loans using other assets. Unlike most other Fed lending facilities, the amount outstanding under TALF steadily rose through 2009. TALF is no longer making new loans, but there are still loans outstanding that were made before the facility ended.

Through September 2013, interest paid on TALF loans was $1.6 billion over the life of the program. By January 2013, assets held by TALF exceeded the loans outstanding. At that point, assets in excess of outstanding loans were used to fully repay the funds lent by the Fed and Treasury to fund TALF loans, with additional profits of $0.4 billion paid to Treasury and $0.05 billion paid to the Fed through June 2013. Loans outstanding were $0.1 billion at the end of September 2013; as those remaining loans are repaid, nine-tenths of any profits will flow to Treasury and one-tenth to the Fed. Through June 2013, there had been no defaults on TALF loans reported.[63] Realized gains already exceed outstanding loans and are likely to rise as remaining loans mature.

American International Group

In the fall of 2008, American International Group (AIG) was a federally chartered thrift holding company regulated by the Office of Thrift Supervision

(OTS) at the holding company level, with a broad range of businesses, primarily insurance subsidiaries, which are state-chartered and state-regulated.[64] Facing losses on various operations, AIG experienced a significant decline in its stock price and downgrades from the major credit rating agencies. These downgrades led to immediate demands for significant amounts of collateral (approximately $14 billion to $15 billion in collateral payments, according to contemporary press reports).[65] As financial demands on the company mounted, bankruptcy appeared a possibility, as had occurred with Lehman Brothers on September 15, 2008. Many feared that AIG was "too big to fail" due to the potential for widespread disruption to financial markets resulting from such a failure.

On September 16, 2008 (prior to the existence of TARP), the Fed announced that it was taking action to support AIG in the form of a secured two-year line of credit with a value of up to $85 billion and a high interest rate. In addition, the government received warrants to purchase up to 79.9% of the equity in AIG. On October 8, 2008, the Fed announced that it would lend AIG up to an additional $37.8 billion against securities held by its insurance subsidiaries.[66]

In early November 2008 (following the creation of TARP), the financial support for AIG was restructured. The restructured financial support consisted of (1) reducing the size of the Fed loan to up to $60 billion, with the term lengthened to five years and the interest rate reduced by 5.5%; purchasing of $40 billion in preferred shares through TARP; and (3) replacing the $37.8 billion loan, with up to $52.5 billion total in asset purchases by the Fed through two limited liability corporations known as Maiden Lane II and Maiden Lane III. The 79.9% equity position of the government in AIG remained essentially unchanged after the restructuring of the intervention.

In March 2009, the assistance was restructured further through (1) a partial payback of the Fed loan through a swap of debt for equity in two AIG subsidiaries worth approximately $25 billion, reducing the maximum to $35 billion; and (2) commitments for additional future TARP purchases of up to $29.8 billion in preferred shares at AIG's discretion, and the conversion of existing shares into shares with optional dividend payments.[67] The Maiden Lane LLCs continued operating under the previous terms, with the actual loans extended to the LLCs totaling $43.9 billion at their peak of the possible $52.5 billion.

In September 2010, AIG and the government announced another restructuring of the government's assistance. This restructuring closed on January 14, 2011. The expressed goal was to simplify the government's interest in AIG and provide for a path for the divestment of the government's stake in AIG. The essence of the plan called for (1) ending the Fed's involvement with AIG through loan repayment and transfer of the Fed's equity interests to the Treasury and (2) converting the government's $49.1 billion in existing preferred shares into common shares, which can then be sold to the public over time. The specific steps involved several interlocking transactions, including the initial public offering (IPO) of a large AIG subsidiary, the sale of several other AIG subsidiaries, and the use of up to approximately $20 billion in TARP funds to transfer equity interests from the Fed to the Treasury. Once these transactions closed, the Treasury held 92% of AIG's common equity (1.66 billion shares) and equity interests in AIG's subsidiaries worth approximately $20.3 billion.

Treasury sold the AIG equity over time, completing sales in December 2012. All of the Federal Reserve loans have been repaid and the assets held in the Maiden Lane LLCs have been sold. The last government-held assets relating to the AIG intervention were TARP warrants which were sold in January 2013.

Table 20 summarizes the support received by AIG from both TARP and the Fed, including current and peak asset holdings, losses or gains, and conditions of the support. Although TARP realized losses on its AIG holdings, these losses were more than offset by income that the Fed earned on its AIG transactions.

Government Sponsored Enterprises[68]

In the summer of 2008, the government sponsored enterprises (GSEs) Fannie Mae and Freddie Mac were experiencing rising yields on debt they were rolling over as a result of investors' concerns about the potential scope of losses on mortgage-backed securities (MBS) they held or guaranteed. Congress enacted the Housing and Economic Recovery Act of 2008 (HERA) in response.[69] HERA created a new regulator, the Federal Housing Finance Agency (FHFA), for Fannie Mae and Freddie Mac. It also included enhanced authorization for the government to take the companies into conservatorship or receivership in case of financial distress, as well as temporary authority to provide unlimited funds to Fannie Mae and Freddie Mac as necessary. There were no specific dollar limits to these purchases or loans, but because the government would borrow to provide the funds, they were in effect subject to the statutory limit on the federal government's debt.

Table 20. AIG Support

	Federal Government				Terms and Conditions			
Program	Latest Asset Holdings	Asset Holdings at Peak	Total Income	Realized Losses(-)	Dividend/ Interest Rate	Warrants/ Equity Interests	Subsequent Conversion	Expiration Date
TARP Systemically Significant Failing Institutions	$0	$67.8 billion (Jan. 2011)	$1.0 billion	-$13.5 billion	10% (dividends paid at AIG's discretion)	warrants for 2% of common shares	$49.1 billion[a] converted to AIG common equity; $20.3 billion converted subsidiary equity	Mar. 2014
Fed Loan to AIG	$0	$90.3 billion loan (Oct. 2008)	$8.2 billion in interest; $17.6 billion equity holding	None	3 month LIBOR+3%	warrants for 79.9% (later reduced to 77.9%) of common shares	Reduced balance by $25 billion in exchange for equity in life insurance subsidiaries	Sept. 2013
Fed Loan for Troubled Asset Purchases	$0	$43.8 billion loans to purchase assets (Dec. 2008)	$9.5 billion	None	LIBOR+1%	none	n/a	None.

Sources: January 31, 2014, TARP Daily Update; May 2013 TARP 105(a) Report; Federal Reserve, statistical release H.4.1, *Factors Affecting Reserve Balances of Depository Institutions and Condition Statement of Federal Reserve Banks*, various dates; Federal Reserve Bank of New York, "Actions Related to AIG," http://www.newyorkfed.org/ aboutthefed/aig/index.html; CBO, *Report on the Troubled Asset Relief Program—May 2013;* SIGTARP, *Quarterly Report to Congress*, September 30, 2010; U.S. Treasury Office of Financial Stability, *Agency Financial Report Fiscal Year 2010*, November 2010; AIG website, "What AIG Owes the U.S. Government," September 30, 2010.

Notes: LIBOR = London Interbank Offered Rate. Table does not include funds borrowed through the Fed's broadly-available Commercial Paper Funding Facility.

a. Includes $1.6 billion in additional preferred shares issued in return for previous conversion of shares paying a mandatory dividend to shares paying an optional dividend.

Table 21. Government Sponsored Enterprise Support

Federal Government					Terms and Conditions		
Program	**Current Asset Holdings**	**Asset Holdings at Peak**	**Total Income**	**Realized Losses(-)**	**Dividend Rate**	**Warrants**	**Expiration Date**
Senior Preferred Stock (Treasury)	$187.5 billion (Dec. 31, 2013)	$187.5 billion	$202.8 billion (as of March 2014)	n/a	2008-2012: 10% dividend; 2012: dividends replaced with "net income sweep"	79.9% of common stock with strike price near zero; $1 billion of liquidation preference	Contracts cannot be amended after end of 2009
Debt Purchases (Fed)	$57.2 billion (Dec. 31, 2013)	$168.9 billion (Mar. 31, 2010)	$12.9 billion (through Sept. 30, 2013)	$0	n/a	none	Purchases completed March 2010

Source: Federal Housing Finance Agency, *Current Data on Treasury and Federal Reserve Purchase Programs for GSE and Mortgage-Related Securities*, August 3, 2013; Federal Reserve, *Monthly Report on Credit and Liquidity Programs and the Balance Sheet*, various dates; Fannie Mae, "Fannie Mae Reports Comprehensive Income of $84.8 Billion for 2013 and $6.6 Billion for Fourth Quarter 2013," press release, February 21, 2014, and Freddie Mac, "Freddie Mac Reports Fourth Quarter and Full-Year 2013 Financial Results," press release, February 27, 2014.

Note: Net income for the GSEs includes the quarterly payments announced on February 21 and 27, 2014, that are scheduled to be transferred to the U.S. Treasury in March 2014.

The continued deterioration of Fannie Mae's and Freddie Mac's financial condition led FHFA to place them in conservatorship on September 7, 2008.[70] FHFA defines conservatorship as "the legal process in which a person or entity is appointed to establish control and oversight of a Company to put it in a sound and solvent condition. In a conservatorship, the powers of the Company's directors, officers, and shareholders are transferred to the designated Conservator."[71]

As part of conservatorship, the firms signed contracts to issue new senior preferred stock to the Treasury, which agreed to purchase up to $100 billion of this stock from each of them to cover realized shortfalls between the GSEs' assets and liabilities.[72] The authority to enter into contracts to provide funds expired on December 31, 2009, but additional funds could be (and were) provided under existing contracts after that date. This $100 billion limit was later raised to $200 billion, and, a week before the authority to sign new contracts expired, the contracts were amended to remove the cap between 2010 and 2012.[73] In exchange, Treasury received 10% dividends on the preferred shares,[74] an undetermined quarterly commitment fee beginning at the end of the first quarter of 2010 (the commitment fee was always waived), warrants giving Treasury the option to purchase 79.9% of the companies' common stock at a nominal cost,[75] and $1 billion of "liquidation preference shares."

FHFA reports that the Treasury had purchased $187.5 billion of preferred shares through the first quarter of 2012. Since then, the GSEs' assets have matched their liabilities and no further preferred share issuance has been needed. Under the existing agreement, the GSEs' profits (after dividend payments) would have accumulated in their coffers.[76] Treasury announced in August 2012 that, "(a)cting upon the commitment ... that the GSEs will be wound down and will not be allowed to retain profits, rebuild capital, and return to the market in their prior form," the preferred share agreements had been amended to replace the dividend and commitment fee with a "net income sweep" that would remit all profits to the Treasury.[77] Regardless of the amount remitted, the terms of the sweep do not allow for a reduction in the preferred shares outstanding. Thus, while Treasury has not recouped any principal, it will have earned a cumulative $202.8 billion in income through the first quarter of 2014 once the latest announced quarterly payments have been transferred to the Treasury.[78]

Between December 2008 and March 2010, the Fed purchased $172.1 billion of bonds issued by the GSEs (of which, $67 billion were issued by Freddie Mac, $67 billion were issued by Fannie Mae, and $38 billion were issued by the Federal Home Loan Banks) as part of its "Large Scale Asset Purchases" (popularly known as quantitative easing).[79] The asset purchases had two goals—to provide support to mortgage markets and to stimulate overall economic conditions.[80] Another effect of these purchases is to reduce the GSEs' borrowing costs, all else equal. As these assets have matured, the Fed has replaced them with Treasury securities or MBS, so its holdings have declined over time, to $57.2 billion as of December 31, 2013. The Fed faces no default risk on its GSE holdings as long as the Treasury continues to stand behind the GSEs, and will not experience capital losses (or gains) as long as it continues to hold the securities to maturity. Through the third quarter of 2013, it had earned $12.9 billion in interest from these securities.

The Federal Reserve and Treasury have also bought MBS guaranteed by Fannie Mae, Freddie Mac, and Ginnie Mae (a government agency) since 2008. Between September 2008 and December 2009, Treasury purchased $220.8 billion of MBS, with peak holdings of $197.6 billion in December 31, 2009.[81] From March 2011 to April 2012, it reduced those holdings to zero.[82] Over the life of the program, Treasury reports that it earned $12 billion in profits, net of expenses.[83] As part of its Large Scale Asset Purchases, the Fed purchased $1.25 trillion in MBS between January 2009 and March 2010, and began to purchase MBS again in September 2012. Unlike purchases of GSE preferred stock or bonds, MBS purchases convey no direct benefit to the GSEs, although they indirectly benefit from Treasury and Fed purchases because they are major holders of MBS and the purchases would be expected to cause the value of the MBS to rise, all else equal.

Until 2013, it was considered doubtful that Treasury would ever receive more from the GSEs than what was outlayed due to the GSEs' "legacy losses" stemming from their concentrated financial exposure to the housing crash. For example, as of the end of FY2012, Treasury had written down the market value of its preferred shares and warrants to $109.3 billion, and booked a $9 billion contingent liability for potential losses on existing business that had not yet been realized.[84] Since then, the financial performance of the GSEs has improved markedly as a result of new business that has yielded lower defaults and higher fees, resulting in quarterly surpluses instead of deficits. In the past four quarters, the GSEs have returned net income of $137.6 billion to Treasury.

Cumulative net income will exceed principal outstanding by $15 billion once quarterly payments announced in February 2014 are made in March 2014. Altogether, the GSEs received $187.5 billion in exchange for preferred shares and have paid $202.8 billion in income on those shares, including the pending March 2014 payments. One issue in the ongoing debate on GSE reform is how to maximize the return on the outstanding government support were the GSEs to be wound down or some of their business or assets transferred to a new private company.

Citigroup

On November, 23, 2008, the Treasury, Federal Reserve, and FDIC announced a joint intervention in Citigroup, which had previously been a recipient of $25 billion in TARP Capital Purchase Program funding.[85] This exceptional intervention to "[support] financial stability" consisted of an additional $20 billion purchase of preferred shares through the TARP Targeted Investment Program and a government guarantee for a pool of $306 billion in Citigroup assets (reduced to $301 billion when the guarantee was finalized on January 16, 2009) through the TARP Asset Guarantee Program, the FDIC, and the Federal Reserve. Citigroup paid the federal government a fee for the guarantee in the form of $4 billion in trust preferred securities paying an 8% dividend rate. The Treasury also received warrants for the purchase of common stock in both of these transactions.

On February 27, 2009, Citigroup and Treasury officials agreed that the Treasury Department would convert $25 billion of its TARP CPP investment in Citigroup preferred stock into Citigroup common stock and cancel the warrants taken by Treasury under the CPP. After this conversion, the U.S. government owned approximately 33.6% (7.7 million shares) of Citigroup common stock. The conversion of preferred shares to common stock worsened the government's priority on Citigroup's assets in the event of liquidation, while improving certain capital ratios for the company and relieving it of the obligation to pay dividends to the government, which it had with the preferred shares. The conversion exposed the government to more potential risk as well as to potential upside reward. The government's preferred shares could only be redeemed at par value, regardless of the performance of the company, while the government's holdings of common stock rose and fell in value based on the market valuation of the company.

Table 22. Citigroup Support

	Federal Government				Terms and Conditions			
Program	**Current Asset Holdings/ Guarantees**	**Asset Holdings/ Guarantees at Peak**	**Total Income**	**Realized Losses(-)**	**Dividend/Fee**	**Warrants**	**Subsequent Conversion/ Amendment**	**Expiration Date**
Capital Purchase Program	$0	$25 billion	$6.9 billion	$0	preferred: 5% dividend for first 5 years, 9% thereafter; common: none	210 million with a strike price of $17.85 per share	Converted preferred shares to common stock, subsequently sold for $31.9 billion.	None, shares outstanding until sold or repurchased.
Targeted Investment Program	$0	$20 billion trust preferred securities (until Dec. 2009)	$1.8 billion	$0	8% dividend	188.5 million with a strike price of $10.61	Converted preferred shares to trust preferred securities.	None, shares or securities outstanding until sold or repurchased.
Asset Guarantee Program	$0	$301 billion (up to $244.8 billion of losses borne by Fed, Treasury and FDIC) (until Dec. 2009)	$4.8 billion	$0	following termination, $2.2 billion in trust preferred securities with 8% dividend	66.5 million with a strike price of $10.61 per share	$1.8 billion canceled upon termination of asset guarantee.	Nov. 2018 (residential assets)/Nov. 2013 (non-residential assets)

Sources: January 31, 2014, Daily TARP Update; October 2011 TARP 105(a) Report; October 2011 TARP Dividends and Interest Report; SIGTARP, *Extraordinary Financial Assistance Provided to Citigroup, Inc.*, January 13, 2011; U.S. Treasury press releases, December 10, 2010, February 5, 2013; Federal Reserve.

Note: Assistance to Citigroup through CPP is also included in the CPP Table. Table does not include funds borrowed from Federal Reserve broadly available emergency liquidity facilities.

Table 23. Bank of America Support

Federal Government					Terms and Conditions		
Program	**Current Asset Holdings/ Guarantees**	**Asset Holdings/ Guarantees at Peak**	**Total Income**	**Realized Losses(-)**	**Dividend Rate/Fee**	**Warrants**	**Expiration Date**
Capital Purchase Program	$0	$25 billion until Dec. 2009[a]	$1.3 billion	$0	5% for first 5 years, 9% thereafter	121,792,790 warrants sold for $0.3 billion.	None, shares outstanding until repurchased.
Targeted Investment Program	$0	$20 billion (until Dec. 2009)	$2.7 billion	$0	8%	150,375,940 warrants sold for $1.25 billion	None, shares outstanding until repurchased.
Asset Guarantee Program[b]	$0	$118 billion (up to $97.2 billion of losses borne by Fed, Treasury and FDIC) (until Sept. 2009)	$425 million termination fee	n/a	n/a	n/a	Jan. 2019 (residential assets)/Jan. 2014 (non- residential assets.

Source: November 2010 TARP 105(a) Report; November 2010 TARP Dividends and Interest Report; Congressional Budget Office, *Budget and Economic Outlook*, January 2010; SIGTARP, *Quarterly Report to Congress*, January 30, 2010; OMB, *Analytical Perspectives, FY2011 President's Budget*, Table 4-7; February 2010.

Notes: Assistance to Bank of America through CPP is also included in the CPP Table. Table does not include funds borrowed from Federal Reserve broadly available emergency liquidity facilities.

a. Of the $25 billion of preferred shares, $10 billion were originally issued by Merrill Lynch, which subsequently merged with Bank of America.

b. Proposed agreement; never finalized.

In December 2009, Citigroup and the Treasury reached an agreement to repay the outstanding $20 billion in preferred securities and to cancel the asset guarantee. As part of this agreement, Treasury agreed to cancel $1.8 billion worth of the $4 billion in trust preferred securities originally paid as a fee for the guarantee. Citigroup repurchased the outstanding AGP trust preferred securities on September 30, 2009. While the asset guarantee was in place, no losses were claimed and no federal funds were paid out.

In April 2010, the Treasury began selling its common share holdings in Citigroup. The shares were sold in tranches through 2010, with the completion of the sales early in December 2010. The average sales price for the Treasury shares was $4.14 per share compared with an initial conversion price of $3.25 per share. The gain from the common stock sales was approximately $6.9 billion. Other gains from the Citigroup assistance included (1) $2.2 billion from the sales of the remaining TARP trust preferred securities granted as a fee from the AGP; (2) $3.1 billion in interest and dividends, (3) $0.3 billion from the sale of warrants; and (4) $0.9 billion for the sale of subordinated notes resulting from the FDIC portion of the asset guarantee; and (5) $50 million termination fee to the Fed for the asset guarantee for a total nominal gain (i.e., not discounted for market risk) from the Citigroup intervention of approximately $13.4 billion.[86]

Bank of America

On January 16, 2009, the Treasury, the Federal Reserve, and the FDIC announced a joint intervention in Bank of America, which had previously been a recipient of $25 billion in TARP Capital Purchase Program funds.[87] "[A]s part of its commitment to support financial market stability,"[88] this exceptional assistance included the purchase of an additional $20 billion of Bank of America preferred shares through the TARP Targeted Investment Program[89] and a joint guarantee on a pool of up to $118 billion of certain Bank of America assets (largely those acquired through its merger with Merrill Lynch). The announced guarantee was to remain in place for 10 years for residential mortgage-related assets and five years for all other assets. Bank of America would have borne up to the first $10 billion of losses on the assets, with subsequent losses split 90% to the government and 10% to Bank of America. Within the government, the losses were to be split between the TARP Asset Guarantee Program, the FDIC, and the Fed. Bank of America was to pay the federal government a fee for the guarantee in the form of $4 billion in preferred stock with an 8% dividend rate and warrants to purchase common stock worth $2.4 billion at the time of the agreement.

Although the asset guarantee was announced in January 2009, a final agreement was never signed. On September 21, 2009, Bank of America announced that it had negotiated a $425 million termination fee that allowed it to withdraw from the Asset Guarantee Program, canceling the warrants and preferred shares issued for the program.[90]

On December 9, 2009, Treasury announced that Bank of America had repurchased the $45 billion in preferred stock previously purchased under TARP. The warrants issued under the CPP and the TIP were sold at auction by the government in March 2010 for approximately $1.6 billion. No government assistance to Bank of America remains outstanding.

CONCLUSION

Interventions to stem the financial crisis were undertaken by the Treasury, the Federal Reserve, and the FDIC, separately and jointly. Because the crisis had many causes and symptoms, the response tackled a number of disparate problems, and can be broadly categorized into programs that increased institutions' liquidity, provided financial institutions with equity to rebuild their capital, purchased illiquid securities, intervened in specific financial markets that had ceased to function smoothly, or prevented the failure of large troubled institutions that some deemed "too big to fail."

The primary goal of the various interventions was to end the financial panic and restore normalcy to financial markets. In this sense, the programs were arguably a success. A goal of intervening at zero cost to the taxpayers was never the best measure of success, because non-intervention would likely have led to a greater loss of economic output that indirectly would have worsened the government's finances. Nevertheless, an important part of evaluating the government's performance is whether financial normalcy was restored at a minimum cost to the taxpayers.

In exchange for its outlays, the government has generally received some combination of financial assets, warrants, and loans that can be sold or require repayment in the future and that have generated income to the government in the form of dividends, fees, and interest.[91] Measuring the cost of the program by the government's cash outlay to initially acquire the financial asset (whether it be a common stock, preferred share, or loan) is misleading because it does not take into account the value of the asset that the government receives in exchange, which gives the government legal claims on the future earnings of the company. The true net cost to the government of these programs is the difference in present value between the initial outlay to acquire or guarantee the asset or make the loan, and the money recouped by the government from income payments and subsequent sale or repayment, taking into account the risks that the government was exposed to in the transaction. Ultimately, the cost to the government will be much smaller than the initial outlay, and if the income payments or the asset's resale price is high enough, the government could ultimately make a profit on these outlays (i.e., the present value of revenues could exceed initial outlays).

Although estimates of the economic profits or losses accruing to the government are not consistently available, on a cash-flow basis, most government interventions—including all Federal Reserve programs—generated positive net income for the taxpayers over the life of the program.[92] Only three interventions generated net losses for the government, two of which were assistance to companies that were not financial firms (the automakers). For most programs where principal is still outstanding (including TARP's Capital Purchase Program and assistance to the GSEs), net income has already exceeded, or is expected to eventually exceed, initial outlays. Altogether, these interventions have yielded tens of billions of dollars of net income for the taxpayers on a cash-flow basis, compared with initial estimates that they would cost taxpayers hundreds of billions of dollars.

Another long-term, and more amorphous, cost may be an increased likelihood of future rescues due to increased private sector risk-taking brought on by the expectation that the government will provide a rescue again. In economic terms, this is generally referred to as "moral hazard," and the problem is particularly acute when assistance is provided to insolvent firms, is provided at below market rates, or is provided on similar terms to both risky and prudent firms.

APPENDIX. HISTORICAL FINANCIAL INTERVENTIONS

Table A-1 presents a brief summary of selected government interventions to assist private firms in past crises, and includes information on the type of assistance, initial outlay, and final cost to the Treasury. The table does not include all historical bank or thrift resolutions that required the use of government funds.

Table A-1. Summary of Major Historical Financial Interventions by the Federal Government

Beneficiary/ Source	Action	Financial Commitment	Final Cost to Treasury
U.S. Airlines P.L. 107-42 (September 22, 2001)	Loan Guarantees	Up to $10 billion	None except implicit value of loan guarantees; under $2 billion in loans made.
Savings and Loan Failures P.L. 101-73 (August 9, 1989)	Savings and Loan Failures and Insolvency of Federal Savings and Loan Insurance Corporation	Full faith and credit backing of Federal Savings and Loan Insurance Corporation	$124 billion to $132 billion.
Farm Credit System P.L. 100-233 (January 6, 1988)	Government-guaranteed bonds issued to assist farmer-owned, federally-chartered lenders	Up to $4 billion in bonds may be issued	$1.26 billion extended, all paid back with interest through assessments on Farm Credit System banks.
Continental Illinois (May-July 1984)	Recapitalization of insolvent bank	$3.5 billion purchase of problem loans, $3.5 billion borrowing from Federal Reserve, $1 billion purchase of preferred shares	$1.1 billion.
Chrysler P.L. 96-185 (January 7, 1980)	Loan Guarantees	Authorized up to $1.5 billion. $1.3 billion used.	$311 million profit from sale of warrants.
New York City P.L. 95-339 (August 9, 1978)	Loan Guarantees	$1.65 billion in guaranteed bonds	None, except the implicit value of loan guarantee.

Beneficiary/ Source	Action	Financial Commitment	Final Cost to Treasury
New York City P.L. 94-143 (December 9, 1975)	Short-Term Loans	$2.3 billion	None, except the implicit cost of the risk of loan.
Penn Central P.L. 93-236 (January 2, 1974)	Loan Guarantees in the wake of Railroad Bankruptcy	$125 million loan guarantees; $7 billion in federal operating subsidies	$3 billion net loss after sale of ownership stake plus the implicit value of loan guarantee.
Lockheed P.L. 92-70 (August 9, 1971)	Loan Guarantees	$250 million of loans guaranteed for five years with three year renewal; guarantee and commitment fees charged	$31 million profit from sale of warrants less the lost value of loan guarantee.

Sources: CRS, U.S. Treasury, Federal Reserve, FDIC, GAO.

End Notes

[1] P.L. 110-343; 12 U.S.C. 5311 *et seq.*

[2] See, for example, the testimony of the Honorable Donald Kohn, Vice Chairman of the Federal Reserve Board in U.S Congress, Senate Committee on Banking, Housing, and Urban Affairs, *American International Group: Examining what went wrong, government intervention, and implications for future regulation*, 111th Cong., 1st sess., March 5, 2009, http://banking.senate.gov/public/index.cfm?FuseAction=Files.View&FileStore_id=aa8bcdf 2-f42b-4a60-b6f6- cdb045ce8141.

[3] See, for example, Taylor, John, *Getting Off Track: How Government Actions and Interventions Caused, Prolonged, and Worsened the Financial Crisis*, Stanford: Hoover Institution, 2009.

[4] By statute, the Congressional Oversight Panel ceased activity in April 2011.

[5] For a comparison to actions taken in other countries, see Luc Laeven and Fabian Valencia, "Systemic Banking Crises Database: An Update," International Monetary Fund, Working Paper WP/12/163, 2012.

[6] For programs that did not raise enough revenue to cover costs, net costs were, in effect, shifted to the taxpayer because the programs were not established with any means to subsequently recoup net costs. Instead, net costs were financed through general revenues.

[7] As discussed above, providing funds to insolvent firms can arguably be justified if preventing those firms from failing avoids further spreading the panic.

[8] See, for example, Dawn Kopecki and Catherine Dodge, "U.S. Rescue May Reach $23.7 Trillion, Barofsky Says," *Bloomberg News*, July 20, 2009, http:// www.bloomberg.com/ apps/news?pid=20601087&sid=aY0tX8UysIaM; "Potential Cost of U.S. Financial Bailout: Over $8 Trillion," *CNBC.com*, November 25, 2008, http://www.cnbc.com/id/ 27912307.

[9] CBO, "Troubled Asset Relief Program," blog post, April 16, 2009, available at http:// cbo.gov/ publication/24884.

[10] Government assistance took many forms, including loans, equity purchases, and guarantees, but in each case, companies entered a financial contract with the legal obligation to reimburse the government. In some cases, contracts were subsequently renegotiated, as discussed below, in ways that may have reduced the return to the government but, on the other hand, may have also made repayment more likely. Depending on the contract, recompense took the form of interest, dividends, capital gains (if any), fees, or warrants. Warrants through the TARP program give the government the option to buy common stock in a company in the future at a predetermined price. If the government does not wish to exercise that option in the future, it can sell the warrants back to the firm or to a third party. If the company's stock price subsequently rises (falls), the value of the warrant rises (falls). Warrants were proposed on the grounds that they would give the government some upside profits if asset prices went up, while limiting the government's exposure (the value of a warrant cannot fall below zero) if asset prices went down.

[11] For the GSE preferred shares held by Treasury, net income will exceed principal outstanding when the GSEs make a quarterly payment of $17.6 billion announced on February 21 and 27, 2014, that is scheduled to be transferred to Treasury in March 2014. Pending quarterly payment announced at Fannie Mae, "Fannie Mae Reports Comprehensive Income of $84.8 Billion for 2013 and $6.6 Billion for Fourth Quarter 2013," press release, February 21, 2014, and Freddie Mac, "Freddie Mac Reports Fourth Quarter and Full-Year 2013 Financial Results," press release, February 27, 2014.

[12] Were the government to sell its remaining Ally Financial equity holdings at the same price it received for previous sales, the transaction would be cash-flow positive. Whether this is still true when the government sell its holdings will depend on market prices at that time.

[13] GAO, in effect, took this approach when it reviewed three early official estimates of TARP subsidies, finding subsidy rates of 18% to 27% for the Capital Purchase Program. It should be noted that the CBO and Treasury estimates reviewed by GAO have subsequently been revised downward significantly, as market rates have returned to more normal levels and defaults have proven smaller than originally anticipated. GAO also compared the fees or rates charged by Federal Reserve and FDIC programs to comparable prices in private markets during the crisis. See Government Accountability Office, *Government Support for Bank Holding Companies*, GAO-14-18, November 2013, at http:// www.gao.gov/ assets/ 660/659004.pdf#page=5&zoom=auto,0,792.

[14] Under the Federal Credit Reform Act, the government counts the cost of government borrowing but does not make any adjustment for risk (which a private creditor would require) when calculating the cost of federal credit programs. For more information, see CRS Report RL30346, *Federal Credit Reform: Implementation of the Changed Budgetary Treatment of Direct Loans and Loan Guarantees*, by James M. Bickley.

[15] Congressional Budget Office, *Report on the Troubled Asset Relief Program—May 2013*. This figure excludes the cost of traditional outlays that carry no obligation to be repaid under the TARP housing programs. By CBO's measure, the auto programs, the CDCI, and AIG generate positive subsidies, while the other programs generate negative subsidies (profits). The CBO number is not comparable to the AIG figure in this report's Table 1 because it

does not include gains from Federal Reserve assistance to AIG. See also Treasury, Office of Financial Stability, *Troubled Asset Relief Program Agency Financial Report Fiscal Year 2013*, December 11, 2013, Table 3, at http://www.treasury.gov/ initiatives/financial-stability/reports/Documents/AFR_FY2013_TARP-12-11-13_Final.pdf.

[16] Preferred stock is an equity instrument, but it does not confer any control over the company and typically has a set dividend rate to be paid by the company; it is similar economically to debt, but accounted for as equity.

[17] All amounts disbursed, outstanding, and recognized as a loss from the U.S Treasury's Daily TARP Update for January 31, 2014.

[18] For more information, see CRS Report R41978, *The Role of TARP Assistance in the Restructuring of General Motors*, by Bill Canis and Baird Webel; CRS Report R41940, *TARP Assistance for Chrysler: Restructuring and Repayment Issues*, by Baird Webel and Bill Canis; and CRS Report R41846, *Government Assistance for GMAC/Ally Financial: Unwinding the Government Stake*, by Baird Webel and Bill Canis.

[19] For more information, see CRS Report R40210, *Preserving Homeownership: Foreclosure Prevention Initiatives*, by Katie Jones.

[20] Daily TARP Update for January 31, 2014.

[21] P.L. 111-203, §1302.

[22] Title VII of the American Recovery and Reinvestment Act of 2009 (P.L. 111-5; 123 Stat. 115).

[23] Special Inspector General to TARP, *Quarterly Report to Congress*, Jan. 29, 2014, p. 58, http:// www.sigtarp.gov/ Quarterly%20Reports/January_29_2014_Report_to_Congress.pdf.

[24] In addition, Treasury has forgone the right to unpaid dividends for 59 banks for which Treasury has sold its holdings to the public.

[25] Two studies have concluded that missed payments are a sign of financial weakness. See Dobrina Georgieva, Linus Wilson "TARP's Dividend Skippers," working paper, Social Science Research Network, August 6, 2010; Linus Wilson "TARP's Deadbeat Banks," working paper, Social Science Research Network, August 15, 2010.

[26] Special Inspector General to TARP, *Quarterly Report to Congress*, January 29, 2014, http://www.sigtarp.gov/ Quarterly%20Reports/January_29_2014_Report_to_Congress.pdf.

[27] Federal Deposit Insurance Corporation, "Legacy Loans Program – Winning Bidder Announced in Pilot Sale," press release, September 16, 2009, http:// www.fdic.gov/ news/news/ press/ 2009/pr09172.html. FDIC reports seven other public-private partnership transactions since 2008, but classifies only the September 2009 transaction as a PPIP transaction.

[28] December 2009 TARP 105(a) Report, pp. 15, 30-32.

[29] U.S. Treasury, *Legacy Securities Public-Private Investment Program Update*, May 8, 2013, p. 3, available at http://www.treasury.gov/initiatives/financial-stability/ reports/ Documents/ PPIP%20Report%20033113%20Final.pdf.

[30] For additional information on this program, see CRS Report R41146, *Small Business Administration 7(a) Loan Guaranty Program*, by Robert Jay Dilger.

[31] This section was prepared with the assistance of Bill Canis, CRS specialist in Industrial Organization and Business. For a comprehensive analysis of federal financial assistance to U.S. automakers, see CRS Report R41940, *TARP Assistance for Chrysler: Restructuring and Repayment Issues*, by Baird Webel and Bill Canis; CRS Report R41846, *Government Assistance for GMAC/Ally Financial: Unwinding the Government Stake*, by Baird Webel and Bill Canis; and CRS Report R41978, *The Role of TARP Assistance in the Restructuring of General Motors*, by Bill Canis and Baird Webel. Statistics in the section are taken from Congressional Oversight Panel, *September Oversight Report: The Use of TARP Funds in the Support and Reorganization of the Domestic Automotive Industry*, September 9, 2009, available at http://cop.senate.gov/documents/cop-090909-report.pdf and from various reports and contracts posted by the U.S. Treasury at http:// www. treasury. gov/initiatives/financial-stability/investment-programs/aifp/Pages/ autoprogram.aspx.

[32] See, for example, Statement by Secretary of the Treasury Henry Paulson in U.S. Congress, House Committee on Financial Services, *Oversight of Implementation of the Emergency Economic Stabilization Act of 2008 and of Government Lending and Insurance Facilities: Impact on the Economy and Credit Availability*, 110th Cong., 2nd sess., November 18, 2008.

[33] P.L. 110-343, Division A, Section 3.

[34] In December 2008, the House of Representatives passed H.R. 7321, authorizing the use of certain Department of Energy funds as bridge loans to GM and Chrysler. Passed by a vote of 237-170, the bill was not acted upon in the Senate.

[35] More detail on all of the facilities discussed in this section of the report can be found in CRS Report RL34427, *Financial Turmoil: Federal Reserve Policy Responses*, by Marc Labonte.

[36] This authority was subsequently amended by P.L. 111-203.

[37] While GAO did not estimate subsidy rates, GAO estimated that the rates charged by the Fed on certain Fed facilities were in many cases lower than the rate for comparable market transactions at the time. However, GAO did not attempt to control for differences in the terms and conditions of Fed transactions compared to market transactions that made Fed transactions less risky, such as the fact that certain Fed loans were over-collateralized and made with recourse and that the Fed had a position senior to other creditors in the event of the borrower's failure. See Government Accountability Office, *Government Support for Bank Holding Companies*, GAO-14-18, November 2013, http:// www.gao.gov/ assets/660/ 659004.pdf#page=5&zoom=auto,0,792.

[38] Transaction records can be accessed at http:// www.federalreserve.gov/ newsevents/ reform_ transaction.htm.

[39] U.S. Government Accountability Office, Federal Reserve System: Opportunities Exist to Strengthen Policies and Processes for Managing Emergency Assistance, GAO-11-696, Jul 21, 2011, http://www.gao.gov/new.items/ d11696.pdf.

[40] Federal Reserve, Office of the Inspector General, *The Federal Reserve's Section 13(3) Lending Facilities to Support Overall Market Liquidity,* Nov. 2010, http:// www.federalreserve.gov/ oig/files/FRS_Lending_Facilities_Report_final- 11-23-10_web.pdf.

[41] As of June 2009, Treasury securities, Agency securities, and Agency-guaranteed mortgage-backed securities were no longer accepted as collateral for the TSLF because the Fed deemed these assets to no longer be illiquid. Few of these assets were posted as collateral when the Fed discontinued their use.

[42] This run is described in greater detail in the section entitled "U.S. Department of the Treasury."

[43] To comply with statute, the CPFF was set up as a special purpose vehicle (SPV) controlled by the Fed that borrowed from the Fed to finance its commercial paper purchases.

[44] For more information, see CRS Report R42150, *Systemically Important or "Too Big to Fail" Financial Institutions*, by Marc Labonte.

[45] Federal Reserve Bank of New York, *Maiden Lane Transactions*, http:// www.newyorkfed.org/ markets/ maidenlane.html.

[46] See the initial announcement at http://www.fdic.gov/news/news/press/2008/pr08100.html. See http://www.fdic.gov/ news/news/press/2008/pr08105.html, which provides further details of the program. For more information, see CRS Report R40843, *Bank Failures and the Federal Deposit Insurance Corporation*, by Darryl E. Getter.

[47] 12 U.S.C. §1823(c)(4)(G)

[48] 12 U.S.C. §1843.

[49] Eligible entities could also opt out of one or both of the program components. As the program was extended, participants were offered the chance to opt out with each extension.

[50] A summary of banks who accessed the DGP can be found in Zoltan Pozsar et al, "Shadow Banking," Federal Reserve Bank of New York, *Staff Report*, no. 458, July 2010, Exhibit 29.

[51] See http:// www.fdic.gov/news/news/press/2009/pr09041.html and hhttp:// www.fdic.gov/ regulations/resources/ TLGP/faq.html.

[52] The text of the final rule establishing the facility is on the FDIC website at http:// www. fdic. gov/news/board/ Oct098.pdf.

[53] See http://www.fdic.gov/regulations/resources/tlgp/index.html.
[54] See http://www.fdic.gov/news/news/financial/2009/fil09048.html.
[55] Section 343 of P.L. 111-203.
[56] In June 2012, the FDIC estimated that TAG-insured deposits averaged 3% of total deposits for the 108 banks that failed between 2011 and the first quarter of 2012. See Letter from Martin J. Gruenberg, FDIC acting chairman, to Honorable Shelley Moore Capito, chairman, Subcommittee on Financial Institutions and Consumer Credit, Committee on Financial Services, House of Representatives, June 29, 2012, at http:// www.aba.com/ Issues/ Index/Documents/ FDICResponsetoCapitoonTAG.pdf.
[57] For more information, see CRS Report R42787, *An Overview of the Transaction Account Guarantee (TAG) Program and the Potential Impact of Its Expiration or Extension*, by Sean M. Hoskins.
[58] FDIC, *Temporary Liquidity Guarantee Program*, http:// www.fdic.gov/ regulations/ resources/ TLGP/index.html.
[59] Figure cited in Fed Chairman Ben Bernanke, "Financial Reform to Address Systemic Risk," speech at the Council on Foreign Relations, March 10, 2009, http:// www. federalreserve. gov/newsevents/speech/bernanke20090310a.htm.
[60] Naohiko Baba, Robert N McCauley, and Srichander Ramaswamy, "US Dollar Money Market Funds and Non-US Banks," *BIS Quarterly Review*, March 2009, http:// www.bis.org/ publ/ qtrpdf/r_qt0903g.pdf.
[61] Board of Governors of the Federal Reserve System, press release, November 25, 2008.
[62] On July 20, 2010, Treasury reduced its loss exposure to $4.3 billion, maintaining the 10% maximum loss exposure in light of the actual loans outstanding when the program ended.
[63] Federal Reserve, *Combined Quarterly Financial Report*, June 30, 2013.
[64] For more information on the federal assistance to AIG, see CRS Report R42953, *Government Assistance for AIG: Summary and Cost*, by Baird Webel.
[65] See, for example, "U.S. to Take Over AIG in $85 Billion Bailout; Central Banks Inject Cash as Credit Dries Up," *Wall Street Journal*, September 17, 2008, pp. A1-A6.
[66] In October 2008, AIG also announced that it had applied to the Fed's broadly available Commercial Paper Funding Facility and was approved to borrow up to $20.9 billion at the facility's standard terms. At its peak use in January 2009, AIG had commercial paper worth $16.1 billion outstanding from the CPFF. AIG continued to access the facility until it expired in February 2010. Over the life of the facility, AIG paid $0.4 billion in interest to the CPFF.
[67] AIG issued $1.6 billion of additional preferred shares to the government in recognition of accrued, unpaid dividends on the initial $40 billion in assistance.
[68] This section prepared with the assistance of N. Eric Weiss, Specialist in Financial Economics. See CRS Report RL34661, *Fannie Mae's and Freddie Mac's Financial Problems*, by N. Eric Weiss.
[69] P.L. 110-289.
[70] For more information see the September 7, 2008, statement by Treasury Secretary Henry Paulson at http://ustreas.gov/press/releases/hp1129.htm; and CRS Report RL34661, *Fannie Mae's and Freddie Mac's Financial Problems*, by N. Eric Weiss and CRS Report RS22950, *Fannie Mae and Freddie Mac in Conservatorship*, by Mark Jickling.
[71] Federal Housing Finance Agency, *Questions and Answers on Conservatorship*, press release, September 7, 2008.
[72] For information about the conservatorship of Fannie Mae and Freddie Mac, see CRS Report RL34657, *Financial Institution Insolvency: Federal Authority over Fannie Mae, Freddie Mac, and Depository Institutions*, by David H. Carpenter and M. Maureen Murphy.
[73] Treasury also agreed to make open market purchases of new Fannie Mae- and Freddie Mac-issued MBS and to create a Government Sponsored Enterprise Credit Facility to provide liquidity to them, secured by MBS pledged as collateral, if the companies had difficulty

borrowing money. The GSE Credit Facility was never formalized or accessed, and expired at the end of 2009.

[74] The agreement called for the dividend rate to rise to 12% if dividends were unpaid; in practice, additional preferred shares were issued so that dividends could be paid on time.

[75] The warrants expire in 2028. Were these warrants exercised, it would have the effect of drastically reducing the value of existing common shares. As a result, share values plummeted after the announcement.

[76] For more information, see Federal Housing Finance Agency, U.S. Treasury Support for Fannie Mae and Freddie Mac," *Mortgage Market Note*, no. 10-1, Jan. 20, 2010.

[77] U.S. Treasury, "Treasury Department Announces Further Steps to Expedite Wind Down of Fannie Mae and Freddie Mac," press release, August 16, 2012. The agreement allows the GSEs to build a capital reserve of $3 billion.

[78] The GSEs announced a quarterly payment of $17.6 billion on February 21 and 27, 2014, that is scheduled to be transferred to Treasury in March 2014. Pending quarterly payment announced at Fannie Mae, "Fannie Mae Reports Comprehensive Income of $84.8 Billion for 2013 and $6.6 Billion for Fourth Quarter 2013," press release, February 21, 2014, and Freddie Mac, "Freddie Mac Reports Fourth Quarter and Full-Year 2013 Financial Results," press release, February 27, 2014.

[79] Data on purchases is available from Federal Housing Finance Agency, *Current Data on Treasury and Federal Reserve Purchase Programs for GSE and Mortgage-Related Securities*, August 3, 2013, http://www.fhfa.gov/webfiles/ 25444/TSYSupport%202013-08-08.pdf.

[80] See CRS Report R42962, *Federal Reserve: Unconventional Monetary Policy Options*, by Marc Labonte.

[81] Data on purchases is available from Federal Housing Finance Agency, *Current Data on Treasury and Federal Reserve Purchase Programs for GSE and Mortgage-Related Securities*, August 3, 2013, http://www.fhfa.gov/webfiles/ 25444/TSYSupport%202013-08-08.pdf.

[82] Data on sales available from U.S. Treasury, Agency MBS Purchase Program, http:// www. treasury.gov/resource- center/data-chart-center/Pages/mbs-purchase-program.aspx.

[83] U.S. Treasury, *The Financial Crisis Five Years Later*, September 2013.

[84] U.S. Treasury, *Financial Report of the U.S. Government for FY2012*, p. 88.

[85] U.S. Treasury, "Joint Statement by Treasury, Federal Reserve, and FDIC on Citigroup," press release hp-1287, November 23, 2008.

[86] U.S. Treasury, "Treasury Prices Sale of Citigroup Subordinated Notes for Proceeds of $894 Million, Providing an Additional Profit for Taxpayers on TARP Citigroup Investment," press release, February 5, 2013, http://www.treasury.gov/press-center/press-releases/ Pages/ tg1841.aspx; U.S. Treasury, "TAXPAYERS RECEIVE $10.5 BILLION IN PROCEEDS TODAY FROM FINAL SALE OF TREASURY DEPARTMENT CITIGROUP COMMON STOCK," press release, December 10, 2010, http:// www.financialstability.gov/ latest/ pr_12102010.html; Federal Reserve, "Support for Specific Institutions," available at http:// www.federalreserve.gov/monetarypolicy/ bst_supportspecific.htm.

[87] As part of this transaction, the government received 121,792,790 with strike price of $30.79.

[88] U.S. Treasury, "Treasury, Federal Reserve, and the FDIC Provide Assistance to Bank of America," press release hp1356, January 16, 2009.

[89] As part of this transaction, the government received 150,375,940 warrants with a strike price of $13.30.

[90] U.S. Treasury, "Asset Guarantee Program," available at http:// www.treasury.gov/ initiatives/ financial-stability/TARP- Programs/bank-investment-programs/agp/Pages/overview.aspx.

[91] HAMP, which was not a program to assist the financial sector, does not generate income for the government although it is part of TARP. In the case of government guarantees, the government has collected fees to offset the potential cost of honoring the guarantee.

[92] A program could be cash-flow positive but still result in economic losses if net income were insufficient to adequately compensate the government for borrowing costs and the risks inherent in the transaction.

In: Federal Interventions in Response ... ISBN: 978-1-63485-347-7
Editor: Alyssa G. Harrington

Chapter 2

THE BUDGETARY IMPACT AND SUBSIDY COSTS OF THE FEDERAL RESERVE'S ACTIONS DURING THE FINANCIAL CRISIS*

Kim Kowalewski and Wendy Kiska

SUMMARY AND INTRODUCTION

The financial system plays a vital role in the U.S. economy. It channels funds from savers to businesses, households, and governments that need money to finance investments and other expenditures, and it provides services that are essential for commercial and financial transactions. When the financial system is functioning smoothly, investors trade securities in liquid markets that provide reliable signals about the values of assets, and loans are readily available to creditworthy borrowers.[1] As the nation's central bank, the Federal Reserve System plays an important role in maintaining the stability and liquidity of the financial system through its conduct of monetary policy and its authority as a supervisor and regulator of banking institutions. (See Box 1 for more information about the Federal Reserve System.)

Over the past several years, the nation has experienced its most severe financial crisis since the Great Depression of the 1930s. Unexpected losses on subprime mortgages (loans made to borrowers with poorer than average credit)

---

* This is an edited, reformatted and augmented version of a report issued by the Congressional Budget Office, May 2010.

as well as heightened uncertainty about how exposed some financial institutions might be to additional losses led to a sharp decline in the liquidity of some markets and the availability of credit. The contraction in lending became more severe as the turmoil spread beyond the subprime mortgage market, several large financial institutions failed, and the economy weakened. Net lending by the private financial sector fell from more than \$3.0 trillion in 2007 to annual rates of about \$1.4 trillion in the fourth quarter of 2008 and \$1.8 trillion in the first quarter of 2009.[2]

In response to that contraction, the Federal Reserve undertook a series of extraordinary actions to stabilize financial markets and institutions. It continued to use its traditional monetary policy tools, but in addition, it created a variety of targeted credit programs to help restore liquidity and confidence to the financial sector. Its actions included:

- Expanding lending to depository institutions—that is, to financial institutions, such as commercial banks and savings and loan associations, whose liabilities largely consist of checking and savings accounts and other deposits;
- Creating new lending programs, or "facilities," for nondepository financial institutions and other participants in the financial markets;
- Purchasing mortgage related securities and medium and long term securities of the U.S. Treasury in the open market to put downward pressure on medium and long term interest rates in the mortgage and debt markets; and
- Extending support to financial institutions whose failures policymakers believed could lead to a systemic collapse of financial markets and institutions.

In effect, the Federal Reserve assumed some of the credit providing functions that participants in the financial markets were unable or unwilling to perform. In doing so, it also assumed significantly more risk of incurring losses than it normally takes on in its operations.

The Federal Reserve's activities during the crisis have had a striking impact on the amount and types of assets that it holds (see Figure 1). In July 2007, before the financial crisis began, the Federal Reserve held about \$900 billion in assets; U.S. Treasury securities accounted for about \$790 billion of that amount. The central bank had acquired those securities during its normal operations in conducting monetary policy—the process of influencing the level of short term interest rates and consequently the pace of U.S. economic activity. (Box 2 on page 6 outlines the basic mechanics of monetary policy.) By the end of 2008, the value of the Federal Reserve's assets had grown to about $2,275 billion; of that amount, loans and other support extended to financial institutions made up $1,686 billion. At the end of 2009, when the turmoil in the financial markets had subsided, the total value of the central bank's assets remained essentially where it was at the end of 2008. The amount of direct loans and other support to financial institutions, though still quite high by historical standards, had fallen markedly by the end of 2009, to about $280 billion, but holdings of mortgage-related securities had risen, to just over $1,000 billion.

The Federal Reserve's activities during the crisis have also led to a marked shift in the composition of the central bank's liabilities (see Figure 2). Before the crisis, the major liability on the Federal Reserve's balance sheet was the amount of currency (Federal Reserve notes) in circulation—about $814 billion as of July 2007. At the end of 2009, the amount of reserves that banks held with the Federal Reserve was the central bank's largest liability. Such reserves have grown from about $6 billion at the end of July 2007 to more than $1,022 billion at the end of 2009; those reserves greatly exceed the amount that banks are required to hold.[3] In effect, the Federal Reserve financed its activities during the crisis primarily by creating bank reserves rather than by issuing more currency or increasing its other liabilities.[4]

The amount and composition of the central bank's assets and liabilities are major determinants of the Federal Reserve's impact on the federal budget. That impact is measured by the central bank's cash remittances to the Treasury, which are recorded as revenues in the budget. (The amount that is remitted is based on the Federal Reserve System's income from all of its various activities minus the costs of generating that income, dividend payments to banks that are members of the Federal Reserve System, and changes in the amount of the surplus that it holds on its books.) For fiscal years 2000 through 2008, annual remittances by the Federal Reserve ranged between $19 billion and $34 billion.

The Congressional Budget Office (CBO) projects that the Federal Reserve's actions to stabilize the financial system will boost its remittances to the Treasury during the next several years. That increase reflects the Federal Reserve's larger portfolio of assets, most of which are likely to earn a great deal more than the amount the system must pay in interest on reserves and its other liabilities. CBO projects that remittances will grow from about $34 billion in fiscal year 2009 to more than $70 billion in fiscal years 2010 and 2011.[5]

Box 1. Background on the Federal Reserve System

The Federal Reserve System is the nation's central bank.[1] It was created by the Congress in 1913 to provide a safer, more flexible, and more stable monetary and financial system. Its duties have expanded to include:

- Conducting monetary policy by influencing the monetary and credit conditions in the economy in pursuit of maximum employment, stable prices, and moderate long term interest rates;
- Supervising and regulating certain banking institutions both to ensure the safety and soundness of the U.S. banking and financial system and to protect the rights of consumers;
- Maintaining the stability of the financial system and containing the risk of a financial crisis; and
- Providing financial services to depository institutions (such as commercial banks, credit unions, and savings and loan associations), the U.S. government, and foreign official institutions. Those services include a major role in operating the nation's payments system—the paper based and electronic mechanisms for moving funds, payments, and money among financial institutions throughout the country.

The Federal Reserve System comprises a board of governors and 12 Reserve Banks—in Atlanta, Boston, Chicago, Cleveland, Dallas, Kansas City, Minneapolis, New York, Philadelphia, Richmond, San Francisco, and St. Louis. (The geographic area that each Reserve Bank serves is known as a Federal Reserve District.) The Board of Governors of the Federal Reserve System is an agency of the federal government whose members are appointed by the President with the advice and consent of the Senate. The board supervises the Reserve Banks, which are the operating arms of the central bank.

The Reserve Banks were established by law as private institutions with certain privileges; however, that legislation restricts them to conducting business only as specified in the Federal Reserve Act.[2]

Nominally, they are owned by their "stockholder," or member, banks. Like those private institutions, the Reserve Banks establish their own compensation and hiring policies (subject to the oversight of the Board of Governors) and pay local property taxes.

Each Reserve Bank has its own board of nine directors who are chosen from outside the bank as provided by law. The Board of Governors appoints three directors to represent the public (they reflect a cross section of business, labor, and consumer interests within the Federal Reserve District); one director is appointed the chairman and another the deputy chairman. The member banks of the Federal Reserve District elect six directors—three to represent them and three to represent the public.

Member banks must hold stock in their regional Federal Reserve Bank in an amount equal to 6 percent of their capital and surplus. Half that amount must be paid in to their Reserve Bank; the other half can be called in by the Board of Governors.[3] The holding of such stock, however, does not carry with it the control and financial interest conveyed to holders of the common stock of for-profit organizations. Rather, it is a legal obligation of Federal Reserve membership, and the stock may not be sold or pledged as collateral for loans, nor may it be purchased by individuals or entities other than member banks. Member banks receive a 6 percent dividend annually on their paid-in stock, as specified by law.

The Federal Reserve System is considered to be an independent central bank because its decisions do not have to be ratified by the President or anyone else in the executive branch of government. Many experts consider that independence important for effective policymaking by central banks.[4] However, the system is subject to Congressional oversight. The Board of Governors must report annually to the Congress on the Federal Reserve's operations and semiannually on its conduct of monetary policy. Other actions and policies are also subject to Congressional scrutiny, and the Chairman and other members of the Board of Governors testify before the Congress frequently.[5]

The Federal Reserve finances its own operations and thus does not rely on Congressional appropriations for funding. It remits its net income from these operations to the Treasury.

1. This box draws on material from Board of Governors of the Federal Reserve System, *The Federal Reserve System: Purposes and Functions*, 9th ed. (2005).
2. Information about the act is available at www. federalreserve.gov/aboutthefed/ fract.htm.
3. The Board of Governors requires each Reserve Bank to maintain a surplus equal to the paid-in capital of its member banks.
4. See, for example, Christopher Crowe and Ellen E. Meade, "The Evolution of Central Bank Governance Around the World," *Journal of Economic Perspectives*, vol. 21, no. 4 (Fall 2007), pp. 69–90.
5. Moreover, the Board of Governors, the Federal Reserve Banks, and the Federal Reserve System as a whole are subject to several layers of audit and review. For example, the financial statements of the Board of Governors and the Reserve banks are audited annually by outside auditors.

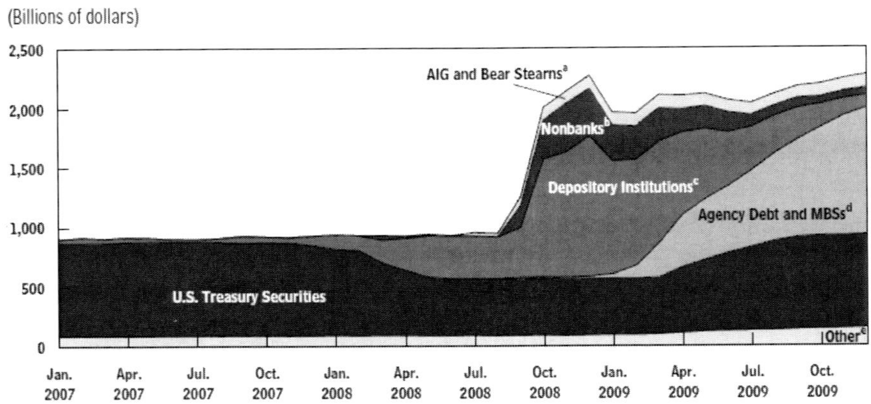

Source: Congressional Budget Office based on data from the Federal Reserve.

Notes: Data are as of the last Wednesday of each month. The last data point is December 30, 2009.

Appendix A contains further information on the programs noted below.

a. For the American International Group (AIG), the total consists of the outstanding balance on the line of credit, the assets of Maiden Lane II and Maiden Lane III, and the Federal Reserve's equity holdings in AIA Aurora Limited Liability Company (LLC) and ALICO Holdings LLC. For Bear Stearns, the total covers the assets of the initial Maiden Lane company.

b. Consists of loans made by the Primary Dealer Credit Facility, the Asset-Backed Commercial Paper Money Market Mutual Fund Liquidity Facility, the Commercial Paper Funding Facility, and the Term Asset-Backed Securities Loan Facility.

c. Comprises loans through the discount window, the assets of the Term Auction Facility, central bank liquidity swaps, and repurchase agreements.

d. Agency debt consists of securities of Fannie Mae, Freddie Mac, and the Federal Home Loan Banks. Agency mortgage-backed securities (MBSs) are securities guaranteed by Fannie Mae, Freddie Mac, and Ginnie Mae.

e. Comprises gold stock, special drawing rights, Treasury currency outstanding, "float," and other assets.

Figure 1. Assets of the Federal Reserve Banks, January 2007 to December 2009.

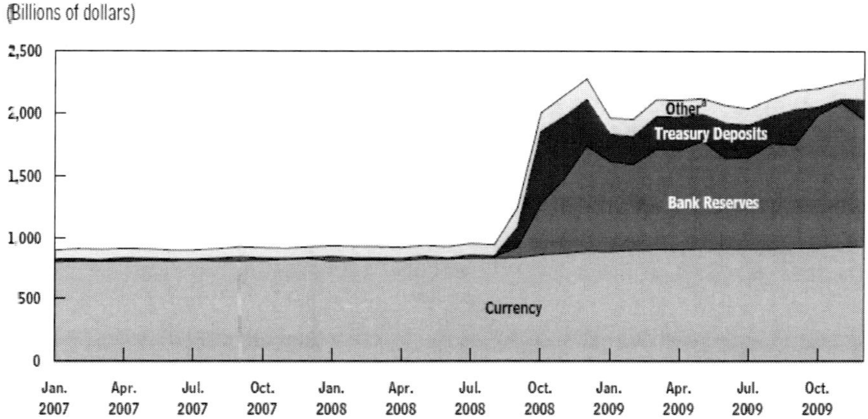

Source: Congressional Budget Office based on data from the Federal Reserve.

Note: Data are as of the last Wednesday of each month. The last data point is December 30, 2009.

a. Comprises reverse repurchase agreements (see Box 2), Treasury cash holdings, deposits other than those of the U.S. Treasury, and other Federal Reserve liabilities and capital.

Figure 2. Liabilities of the Federal Reserve Banks, January 2007 to December 2009.

Projections of the Federal Reserve's remittances to the Treasury over the next few years, however, are more uncertain than projections made in the past. The system's asset holdings are now riskier, exposing the central bank to a considerably greater possibility of losses than its usual holdings of Treasury securities do. Moreover, the risk of losses from default associated with the amounts of the remittances is asymmetric. The chances are great that the Federal Reserve will remit slightly more than the amounts CBO expects. But there is also a small chance that it will remit much less—or even nothing—if serious problems reemerge in the financial markets or the economy greatly weakens again.

Measuring the impact of the Federal Reserve System's actions by the magnitude of its cash remittances to the Treasury fails to account for the cost of the risks to tax payers from those actions. When the Federal Reserve invests in a risky security, it increases its expected net earnings because the return it anticipates on that security exceeds the interest rate it pays on the debt used to fund the purchase. If the Federal Reserve purchases the security at a fair market price, equivalent to what private investors would have paid, then the purchase creates no economic gain or loss for taxpayers; the price compensates the central bank for the risk it has assumed. By contrast, if the Federal Reserve purchases a risky security for more than the amount that private investors would have paid, it gives a subsidy to the seller of the security, creating an economic loss, or cost, for taxpayers.

The economic cost of the Federal Reserve System's actions to stabilize the financial markets—which incorporates the risks to taxpayers—can be estimated using "fair value" subsidies. Fair value in many instances corresponds to market value; it is defined as the price that would be received by selling an asset in an orderly transaction between market participants on a designated measurement date.[6] Subsidies estimated on a fair value basis provide a more comprehensive measure of cost than do estimates made on a cash basis: They take into account the discounted value of all future cash flows associated with a credit obligation, and they include the cost of bearing risk.[7] CBO and the Administration's Office of Management and Budget (OMB) use a conceptually similar subsidy measure, as specified by the Emergency Economic Stabilization Act of 2008, to estimate the budgetary cost of the Troubled Asset Relief Program, or TARP.[8] (CBO calls such subsidies "fair value" in part to distinguish them from subsidies calculated through the method specified by the Federal Credit Reform Act of 1990 and used by CBO and OMB to estimate the budgetary cost of federal credit programs.)[9]

In CBO's estimation, the fair value subsidies conferred by the Federal Reserve System's actions to stabilize the financial markets totaled about $21 billion (see Table 1 for details). The subsidies are estimated as of the date of inception of the main programs that the central bank put in place—when the major economic commitments occurred—and they incorporate CBO's projections of all future cash flows over the life of those facilities, the uncertainty surrounding the flows, and the expected rate of return that investors would have required for taking on the same obligations. The gains or losses that will ultimately be realized from the Federal Reserve's activities will almost certainly deviate from CBO's estimates of the fair value subsidies those actions provided. Such forward looking estimates are based on averages over many possible future outcomes, whereas realized gains or losses reflect a particular outcome.

Box 2. Monetary Policy

A primary function of the Federal Reserve System is the conduct of monetary policy. The central bank is charged by the Congress to use monetary policy "to promote effectively the goals of maximum employment, stable prices, and moderate long term interest rates," as required by the Federal Reserve Act.[1] Since the mid 1980s, the central bank has carried out that directive on a day to day basis primarily by targeting the federal funds rate—the interest rate that banks charge each other for overnight loans of their spare reserves.

The Federal Reserve influences the federal funds rate by changing the amount of available funds in the federal funds market. Before the financial crisis, the central bank altered the amount of funds primarily by buying and selling U.S. Treasury securities and by participating in repurchase and reverse repurchase agreements.[2] Those activities have direct effects on the federal funds rate and indirect effects on other interest rates in the financial markets. For example, when the Federal Reserve wants to lower the federal funds rate, it buys Treasury securities from dealers in the open market. (To raise the federal funds rate, it sells securities.) Those transactions add to the supply of bank reserves that banks can lend in the overnight market—because the dealers deposit the proceeds of such sales in their banks—thereby lowering the federal funds rate and adding to the Federal Reserve's holdings of Treasury securities. The central bank can also increase (or decrease) the amount of reserves by carrying out a repurchase (or a reverse repurchase) agreement.

The central bank has traditionally used two other methods as well for adjusting the amount of reserves in the banking system, although those methods are less useful for day to day adjustments of the federal funds rate. First, the Federal Reserve can increase the amount of reserves by making loans through its so called discount window, a facility that makes collateralized loans (typically overnight) to banks and other depository institutions. However, the Federal Reserve has discouraged banks from using the discount window in situations that do not constitute an emergency. Consequently, the amount of discount window lending is typically very small.

A second method that the central bank can use to adjust reserves is to change its reserve requirements— which specify the amount of reserves that depository institutions must hold at the Federal Reserve Banks. However, frequent alterations in the requirements are impractical.

Recently, the Federal Reserve was granted the authority to pay interest on bank reserves, giving it a new tool with which to influence the level of reserves in the system as well as interest rates in the broader financial market.

1. Information about the Federal Reserve Act of 1913 is available at www. federalreserve.gov/aboutthefed/fract.htm. Further discussion of the Federal Reserve's monetary policy role is at www.federalreserve.gov/ generalinfo/faq/faqmpo.htm.
2. Repurchase agreements are similar to collateralized loans. In a repurchase agreement, a primary dealer (a bank or another financial institution that meets the central bank's capital and other requirements) *sells* high quality securities, such as Treasury securities, to the Federal Reserve and agrees to buy them back on a set date and for a set price. In a reverse repurchase agreement, a dealer *buys* high quality securities from the Federal Reserve and pledges to sell them back to the central bank on an agreed upon date and at an agreed upon price.

In total, the fair value subsidies that CBO has estimated are modest when compared, for instance, with CBO's estimate of the $189 billion subsidy provided by the TARP at its inception—even though most of the central bank's facilities were introduced near the height of the crisis, when the price of risk was substantial and the probability of default was elevated.[10] The subsidies' relatively small magnitude reflects the fact that the Federal Reserve's potential for losses was limited in most instances by requirements for borrowers to provide collateral, by guarantees from the Treasury under the TARP and from the Federal Deposit Insurance Corporation (FDIC), or by various restrictions on the programs. Furthermore, some of the assistance that the Federal Reserve provided involved no subsidies because the transactions were con ducted on a fair value basis or at prices determined in competitive auctions—meaning that the central bank was fully compensated for the risks it assumed.

CBO's estimates of the economic subsidies that the Federal Reserve has provided are highly uncertain. The estimates necessarily rely on judgments about the probability that the crisis would have deepened or abated, about the sums that might be borrowed and their associated interest rates at such times, and about the severity of losses. Uncertainty also surrounds the discount rates used in CBO's calculations, but that effect is mitigated by the short time over which most of the facilities were scheduled to operate. Indeed, most programs have already been ended.

Table 1. Fair-Value Subsidies Arising from the Federal Reserve's Actions during the Financial Crisis

Program/Activity	Inception Date	Subsidy at Inception[a] (Billions of dollars)
Lending to Depository Institutions		
Term Auction Facility	December 12, 2007	0
Repurchase agreements	Ongoing	0
Reciprocal currency arrangements	December 12, 2007	n.a.
Lending to Nondepository Financial Institutions and Other Market Participants		
Primary Dealer Credit Facility	March 17, 2008	0
Term Securities Lending Facility	March 27, 2008	0
Asset-Backed Commercial Paper Money Market Mutual Fund		
Liquidity Facility	September 22, 2008	2
Money Market Investor Funding Facility	October 21, 2008	0
Commercial Paper Funding Facility	October 27, 2008	2
Term Asset-Backed Securities Loan Facility	March 3, 2009	13
Direct Purchases of Securities	Ongoing	0
Support for Systemically Important Financial Institutions[b]		
Maiden Lane LLC	March 14, 2008	0
Maiden Lane II LLC	October 31, 2008	0
Maiden Lane III LLC	October 31, 2008	0
AIG revolving credit facility	September 16, 2008	2
Citigroup	November 23, 2008	2
Bank of America	January 16, 2009	1
Total		**21**

Source. Congressional Budget Office.

Notes: Subsidies estimated on a fair-value basis, unlike estimates made on a cash basis, take into account the discounted value of all future cash flows associated with a credit obligation and include noncash costs, such as that for bearing risk. For further information on the programs and activities listed above, see Appendix A.

n.a. = not applicable; LLC = limited liability company; AIG = American International Group.

a. Numbers in the column do not add to the total because of rounding.

b. The Maiden Lane LLC was established in conjunction with the sale of the investment bank Bear Stearns to JPMorgan Chase & Company. Maiden Lanes II and III were established to provide support to AIG.

It bears emphasizing that CBO's fair value estimates address the costs but not the benefits of the Federal Reserve's actions. In CBO's judgment, if the Federal Reserve had not strategically provided credit and enhanced liquidity, the financial crisis probably would have been deeper and more protracted and the damages to the rest of the economy more severe. Measuring the benefits of the Federal Reserve's interventions in avoiding those worse outcomes is much more difficult than estimating the subsidy costs of the interventions, and CBO has not attempted to do so. It is likely, though, that the benefits of the Federal Reserve's actions to stabilize the financial system exceeded the relatively small costs reported here for fair value subsidies.

ACTIONS BY THE FEDERAL RESERVE TO ADDRESS THE FINANCIAL CRISIS

In reacting to the recent turmoil in the financial markets, the Federal Reserve used its traditional tools for implementing monetary policy as well as new facilities to help restore liquidity and confidence within the financial markets and among institutions. Using its traditional tools, the Federal Reserve expanded lending to depository institutions and lowered its target for the overnight federal funds rate to almost zero to put downward pressure on market interest rates. The Federal Reserve also created new facilities to provide liquidity to nondepository financial institutions and other market participants and purchased mortgage related securities and medium and long term U.S. Treasury securities in the open market. It also extended direct loans and other support to certain "systemically important" financial institutions (institutions whose financial problems during the crisis were believed to seriously threaten the stability of the financial system as a whole).

Expanded Lending to Depository Institutions

In its earliest actions to address the financial crisis, the Federal Reserve focused on providing liquidity to depository institutions, generally by using existing programs. It expanded opportunities for borrowing from its discount window, which serves as a backup source of liquidity for individual depository institutions, by reducing the cost of loans and extending their maximum maturity from over-night to 90 days. And it increased its use of repurchase agreements (short term collateralized loans) to add liquidity to the banking system. Other actions included expanding its currency swap lines with foreign central banks to make additional dollar denominated funding available to foreign commercial banks and creating the Term Auction Facility (TAF) to provide longer term loans to depository institutions at market determined rates of interest.[11] (Appendix A provides additional details on those and other actions by the Federal Reserve to meet the crisis in the banking system.) Taken together, the out-standing amount of lending through those programs rose from about $19 billion at the end of July 2007 to a peak of $1,201 billion in December 2008. By the end of 2009, however, lending to depository institutions had fallen to about $106 billion (see Figure 1 on page 4).

New Liquidity Programs for Nondepository Financial Institutions and Other Market Participants

As the crisis deepened, the Federal Reserve created new programs to provide liquidity directly to other financial institutions and participants in the financial markets—in particular, primary dealers, money market mutual funds, and participants in the markets for commercial paper and asset backed securities.[12] Those institutions and participants directly or indirectly provide a significant amount of credit to consumers and businesses. In normal times, the Federal Reserve could have provided liquidity to many such institutions indirectly by providing additional reserves to banks, which could then have lent the funds to the institutions. However, the curtailment of banks' lending activities during the crisis blocked the normal channels through which the Federal Reserve could affect the financial markets and the economy more broadly. Consequently, the central bank created:

- The Primary Dealer Credit Facility and the Term Securities Lending Facility (TSLF), to provide primary dealers with access to short term liquidity;
- The Asset Backed Commercial Paper Money Market Mutual Fund Liquidity Facility (AMLF) and the Money Market Investor Funding Facility (MMIFF), to ease the liquidity problems of money market funds;[13]

- The Commercial Paper Funding Facility (CPFF), to support the issuance of commercial paper by buying highly rated offerings; and
- The Term Asset Backed Securities Loan Facility (TALF), to encourage the issuance of asset backed securities and hence increase the availability of credit to businesses and households.

Total lending by those facilities (excluding the TSLF, which lent securities rather than cash) peaked at over $400 billion in late November 2008 and then declined to approximately $62 billion at the end of 2009 (see Figure 1 on page 4). In October 2008, the TSLF had loans totaling close to $200 billion; by August 2009, it had no outstanding loans.

Open-Market Purchases of Securities

The Federal Reserve began purchasing medium and long term securities (those with maturities of 2 to 10 years and more than 10 years, respectively) in the open market in late 2008 in an effort to lower medium and long term interest rates, including mortgage rates, and thereby support the housing market and the broader economy. The Federal Reserve stated that it would purchase as much as $200 billion (later reduced to $175 billion) in debt securities—known as agency debt—from Fannie Mae, Freddie Mac, and the Federal Home Loan Banks, as well as up to $1,250 billion in mortgage backed securities guaranteed by Fannie Mae, Freddie Mac, and Ginnie Mae—known as agency MBSs.[14] (A mortgage backed security is a claim on the cash flows of a pool of mortgages.) By the end of 2009, the Federal Reserve owned $160 billion of agency debt and $908 billion of agency MBSs. Over the course of that year, the central bank had also purchased $300 billion of medium and long term Treasury securities.

Support for Systemically Important Financial Institutions

In conjunction with the Treasury and the Federal Deposit Insurance Corporation, the Federal Reserve provided substantial additional support to four institutions whose financial problems during the crisis were believed to seriously threaten the financial system's stability.

- The Federal Reserve created the Maiden Lane facility in conjunction with the sale of the troubled investment firm Bear Stearns to the bank JPMorgan Chase & Company. The facility, which is structured as a limited liability company, received financing from the Federal Reserve to purchase about $30 billion of Bear Stearns' assets, which were residential and commercial mortgage loans and other mortgage related assets.[15] (In essence, the Federal Reserve owns those underlying assets.)
- The Federal Reserve also provided assistance to American International Group (AIG), a large financial institution with businesses in insurance and other financial products. The assistance mainly included a line of credit and the creation of the Maiden Lane II and Maiden Lane III facilities, which own a portion of AIG's asset backed securities financed by the central bank. (Here again, the Federal Reserve effectively owns the underlying assets.)[16] Maiden Lane II holds residential MBSs, whereas Maiden Lane III holds col lateralized debt obligations—that is, securities backed by a pool of various assets.
- The Federal Reserve, together with the Treasury's Troubled Asset Relief Program and the FDIC, provided guarantees on certain assets owned by the commercial banks Citigroup and Bank of America. Under the agreements, the Federal Reserve would provide so called contingent loans to the banks in the event that losses on the assets exceeded the amounts covered by the TARP and the FDIC.[17] By December 2009, those agreements had been terminated.

THE PROJECTED IMPACT OF THE FEDERAL RESERVE'S ACTIONS ON THE FEDERAL BUDGET

In the course of its regular activities, the Federal Reserve generates a stream of income in excess of its expenses and other payments that flows to the Treasury and reduces the budget deficit. Ordinarily, most of that income arises from the interest paid on Treasury securities that the Federal Reserve acquires in carrying out monetary policy. The central bank's other major sources of income are the interest on its investments in foreign currency and on loans to depository institutions, and the fees it receives for services it provides to such institutions—such as check clearing, transfers of funds, and automated clearinghouse operations. The central bank's income minus its expenses, the dividends paid to member banks, and additions to its surplus account is remitted to the Treasury and appears in the federal budget as revenues— specifically, the remittances are labeled "deposits of earnings of the Federal Reserve System" under the category "miscellaneous receipts."[18] Annual remittances by the Federal Reserve during fiscal years 2000 to 2008 ranged between $19 billion and $34 billion.

The Federal Reserve's actions to stabilize the financial markets are likely to significantly increase the amount of its remittances over the next few years. CBO incorporates estimates of the Federal Reserve's annual remittances in its 10 year baseline projections of the federal budget. In CBO's estimation, remittances will more than double from about $34 billion in fiscal year 2009 to over $70 billion in fiscal years 2010 and 2011 but then taper off to $41 billion in 2013.[19] The near term increase in remittances reflects CBO's expectations that the size of the Federal Reserve's asset portfolio will remain unusually large for the next few years and that the return on those assets will exceed the interest rate that the Federal Reserve pays on reserves. The projected decline in remittances between 2011 and 2013 reflects CBO's assumptions that short term interest rates will be higher and the Federal Reserve will be reducing its asset holdings, primarily its holdings of agency MBSs. After 2013, CBO projects, annual remittances will rise gradually to $55 billion in 2020, in line with growth in the overall economy, and derive increasingly from interest receipts on the central bank's holdings of Treasury securities.

The expansion of the central bank's activities has also significantly increased the uncertainty associated with its remittances over the next several years. That is because some of the Federal Reserve's new credit activities entail considerably more risk of losses—from increased interest rates, defaults, or prepayment of the mortgages backing its MBSs—than its normal asset holdings entail. Moreover, the Maiden Lane facilities are a source of greater expected volatility in the central bank's remittances because changes in the fair values of the facilities' assets flow through to the Federal Reserve's reported earnings.[20] In addition, the risk of default associated with the Federal Reserve's remittances is asymmetric, with a large probability of slightly more in remittances than the amount CBO expects but a small probability of much less in the event that serious problems reemerge in the financial markets or the economy goes into another downturn.[21]

Effects of the Federal Reserve's Liquidity Programs and Purchases of Securities

CBO's projections of the Federal Reserve's annual remittances to the Treasury depend on projections of the size and composition of the central bank's portfolio of assets and the returns expected from it. Those estimated returns depend in turn on projections of economic activity, the stance of monetary policy, and developments in the financial markets. CBO expects that the Federal Reserve's increased income over the next several years will largely derive from its substantial holdings of agency debt and agency MBSs. (CBO's projections reflect only a small amount of income from the emergency liquidity facilities that the central bank established because most of those facilities were winding down and ceasing operation during the first half of fiscal year 2010.) Indeed, CBO expects the Federal Reserve to earn more than $45 billion annually in interest income from its holdings of agency debt and agency MBSs in fiscal years 2010 and 2011, accounting for about two thirds of its income. Offsetting some of that income, however, will be interest that the Federal Reserve pays on bank reserves. The interest rate on reserves is a short term rate; CBO expects short term interest rates to rise as the economy continues to recover but to remain lower than the interest rates on the Federal Reserve's longer term assets.

Size of the Federal Reserve's Asset Portfolio. In its latest set of baseline economic projections issued in January 2010, CBO concluded that the economy would grow at a subdued pace over the next few years.[22] That pace in part reflects CBO's assessment that financial systems both in the United States and abroad will take some time to heal. CBO believes that in those circumstances, the Federal Reserve will implement monetary policy by slowly reducing the amount of liquidity in the financial markets over the next two years, while the economy is recovering from the recession. CBO has thus assumed that the central bank will carefully reduce the size of its asset portfolio, raise the interest rate that it pays on reserves (which will lead to higher short term interest rates in the financial markets), and otherwise adjust the amount of its other liabilities to manage the reduction in liquidity. The total amount of the Federal Reserve's assets in CBO's projection begins to fall later this year, but it remains above $2 trillion through the early part of 2012.

The Federal Reserve faces a considerable challenge in reducing the amount of liquidity in the financial system in a way that supports the economic recovery but avoids creating either inflationary or deflationary conditions. An overly slow reduction in the amount of liquidity would keep interest rates low for too long, overstimulating economic activity and contributing to higher inflation. Conversely, an overly rapid reduction in liquidity would raise interest rates too quickly, possibly stifling the economic recovery and creating deflationary conditions. Balancing those risks and choosing a course of action are difficult because the Federal Reserve must of necessity act on the basis of incomplete information and uncertain forecasts, at times in response to rapidly changing circumstances.

The unprecedented nature of recent economic developments and the central bank's response to those occurrences suggest that the potential for error in predicting monetary policy is greater than usual. When the Federal Reserve begins to withdraw excess liquidity from the financial markets, it can choose different combinations of reducing its asset holdings and raising the interest rate that it pays on bank reserves. The central bank may decide to sell some of its assets—in particular, its agency MBSs—or it may simply allow those MBS holdings to decline as the underlying mortgages are repaid. The speed with which the Federal Reserve reduces those holdings, however, will probably depend on conditions in the housing market and in the market for those securities—a faster recovery of such markets would encourage the central bank to reduce its MBS holdings more quickly.

The Federal Reserve could also tighten monetary policy by increasing the interest it pays on excess reserves, thereby encouraging banks to continue holding large amounts on deposit. Such a policy would effectively neutralize those funds (and the liquidity they represent) because banks would not be loaning them out to the private sector.

Nevertheless, because the Federal Reserve has never had to manage such a large reduction in its asset holdings, it is difficult to forecast the path that the central bank will take. Any of the measures to reduce liquidity in the financial markets would reduce the central bank's net interest income; the amount of the reduction would vary with the course and extent of the action taken.

Composition of the Federal Reserve's Asset Portfolio. CBO expects that the Federal Reserve's holdings of agency debt and agency MBSs will account for a significant share of its asset portfolio over the next few years. By the second half of the 2010–2020 projection period, the Federal Reserve's asset holdings will largely consist of Treasury securities, in CBO's view.

Expected Returns on the Federal Reserve's Agency Debt and Agency MBSs. CBO used market data to estimate the rates of return on the Federal Reserve's purchases of agency debt and agency MBSs. Specifically, it computed average returns for the central bank's holdings on the basis of the characteristics of the securities that the Federal Reserve purchased and the market interest rates for those securities at the time they were acquired.

Effects of Support for Systemically Important Institutions

CBO estimates that the Federal Reserve's support of institutions whose failures might have threatened the stability of the financial system will increase its net income by about $17 billion over the fiscal year 2010–2020 period.[23] That figure consists of a projected return of $8 billion on the three Maiden Lane facilities and interest of $9 billion on the line of credit to AIG. The contingent loan arrangements with Citigroup and Bank of America have been terminated.

The Maiden Lane Facilities. The effect of the Maiden Lane facilities on the Federal Reserve's remittances to the Treasury is measured by the facilities' net income, which comprises both realized and unrealized gains and losses on the facilities' portfolios of assets (see Appendix B). (Unrealized gains and losses are determined by changes in the fair values of those assets.) That definition of net income follows from the particular accounting standards that the Federal Reserve uses for those facilities.

CBO anticipates that over the lifetimes of the Maiden Lane facilities (that is, from the inception of the programs through fiscal year 2020), the Federal Reserve will gain $200 million in income from its investment in the initial Maiden Lane company (related to the Bear Stearns trans action) and $2 billion each from its investments in Maiden Lane II and Maiden Lane III (both related to support for AIG). Those estimates include losses that have already occurred. As of September 30, 2009, the value of the assets in all of the Maiden Lane facilities had dropped by $7.4 billion. Approximately half that loss—$3.7 billion—has been allocated to the Federal Reserve.[24]

CBO expects positive returns from all three facilities because the assets were purchased at their fair values.[25] CBO assumed that each facility's portfolio would have an expected return of 6.5 percent and that the assets had terms of between 2½ and 5 years. (CBO based its assumption about expected returns on those earned by securities bought and sold in the private markets.)

Of course, the returns realized on asset backed securities such as those in the Maiden Lane portfolios could deviate significantly from what is expected, given the uncertainty about the returns on the underlying assets. The actual outcomes from the Maiden Lane investments depend on what happens to the economy, and the Federal Reserve could experience significant losses if the economy worsens. Also a possibility, though, is that it could reap large gains if the market for asset backed securities turns around more quickly than has been anticipated.

Line of Credit for the American International Group. CBO estimates that the Federal Reserve will earn almost $12 billion in interest over the lifetime of the loans made to AIG under its line of credit. (The central bank had earned $3 billion of that amount before the start of fiscal year 2010.) That estimate is based on CBO's projections of the interest rate on the loan (the three month Libor plus 3 percentage points), the loan's outstanding balance, and the fee of 0.75 percent on the unused portion of the line of credit.[26] CBO also judged that default losses on the line of credit would be negligible (because the loan is collateralized by all of the assets of AIG and its subsidiaries) and that the facility would cease operating, on schedule, in August 2013.

Contingent Loans to Bank of America and Citigroup. CBO's current projections do not incorporate the contingent lines of credit offered to Bank of America and Citi group. In September 2009, Bank of America terminated its provisional loan agreement with the Treasury, the FDIC, and the Federal Reserve and paid an exit fee of $57 million to the central bank. In December of that year, Citigroup also terminated its agreement with those parties and paid an exit fee of $50 million.

ESTIMATES OF FAIR-VALUE SUBSIDIES FROM THE FEDERAL RESERVE'S ACTIONS

From an economic perspective, the higher rate of return that CBO expects on the Federal Reserve's riskier assets is compensation for the central bank's increased exposure to the risks associated with those investments and not a true gain of value to the Treasury. A more comprehensive measure of the costs of the Federal Reserve's activities during the recent crisis that takes the value of risk bearing into account is the economic, or fair value, subsidies that the central bank provided to financial institutions in the form of credit and guarantees. The concept of fair value has been increasingly used to account for financial obligations in the private sector; it is defined as the price that would be received by selling an asset in an orderly transaction between willing market participants on a specified measurement date.

In general, a fair value subsidy arises whenever the Federal Reserve accepts terms on the financing it is providing that are less stringent than the terms that investors would demand for taking on comparable risks.[27] The cost of such subsidies is borne by taxpayers because the credit assistance that the Federal Reserve chooses to provide affects the size and timing of its remittances to the Treasury. For instance, the central bank's activities create a fair value subsidy when the principal amount of a loan it makes exceeds the value to private investors of the promised repayments from the loan. But when the Federal Reserve acquires assets at their fair values, as it effectively did through its Maiden Lane facilities, it does not confer subsidies on the sellers of those assets because the assets' purchase prices represented fair compensation for the risks that the central bank was assuming. Similarly, the Federal Reserve's purchases of agency debt, agency MBSs, and long term Treasury securities do not give rise to fair value subsidies because those transactions all occurred in the open market.

Economic subsidies can be defined more or less broadly. For this analysis, CBO estimated only those subsidies that arose from activities of the Federal Reserve that exposed it to market risk—the risk that defaults will be unusually high during times of stress in the economy. Many of the central bank's actions that were aimed at increasing liquidity and lowering interest rates involved a negligible risk of losses from default. However, some of the Federal Reserve's actions provided financial institutions with credit at a price lower than that available from the markets and thus could be viewed as having conferred a subsidy. For instance, the Federal Reserve's actions through its Term Auction Facility appear to have involved very little default risk because the loans extended through the TAF were highly secured. However, the terms that the central bank offered on those loans were probably more favorable to the borrowing banks than the terms they could have obtained privately, as evidenced by the large volume of lending (over $450 billion) through the TAF at the height of the crisis. As a practical matter, it would be extremely difficult to estimate those more broadly defined subsidies, and CBO has not attempted to do so.

The central bank's interventions took a number of forms that exposed it to varying degrees of risk. CBO used several modeling approaches to estimate the fair value of the assets of the different facilities, but all relied on data about market prices to draw inferences about the cost of the risks being assumed. On the basis of those models, CBO estimated that when the programs were introduced, the Federal Reserve conferred fair value subsidies totaling approximately $21 billion. (Most of that amount—an estimated $13 billion—is attributable to the Term Asset Backed Securities Loan Facility.) The Federal Reserve will realize actual gains or losses from those programs that will almost certainly differ from CBO's estimates of the fair value subsidies, which reflect the wide range of outcomes that were possible when the programs were initiated.

Methodological Considerations

The idea that investors require compensation for assuming certain risks is central to the concept of fair value. Investors require a return that compensates them for the "time value of money"—that a dollar today is worth more than a dollar in the future because it can earn interest— and that covers the losses expected from default. In addition, investors require a "risk premium"—an expected return in excess of the risk free rate—that compensates them for bearing certain types of risk, such as market risk.[28] CBO and the Office of Management and Budget use a subsidy measure that includes the cost of market risk to estimate the budgetary cost of the Troubled Asset Relief Program, as specified by the Emergency Economic Stabilization Act of 2008.[29] CBO calls such subsidies fair value subsidies in part to distinguish them from those that CBO and OMB calculate to estimate the budgetary cost of federal credit programs, as specified in the Federal Credit Reform Act of 1990. Subsidies calculated under the requirements of that law take into account the time value of money and expected losses but not the cost of market risk. Specifically, the act specifies that expected cash flows should be discounted at the interest rates of maturity matched Treasury securities. As a result, such subsidy measures do not include a charge for the cost of risk.

The fair value of an asset is generally the same as its market price when the asset is traded in a market that is functioning normally. However, when few or no similar private transactions occur or when there is no comparable private contract, then fair values must be approximated. During the financial crisis, private investors clearly viewed the risk of default as extremely costly, as evidenced by the marketwide decline in the price of securities that carried even moderate amounts of default risk. For most of the Federal Reserve's programs that are evaluated here, CBO used comparable market interest rates to impute market risk premiums and thus calculate the fair value subsidies that the central bank was providing. When comparable rates were not available, CBO approximated risk premiums by using historical relationships and available market data on related transactions.

In valuing assets, fair value accounting does not generally distinguish between the effect of market risk and the effect of liquidity risk—the risk that selling an asset in an inactive market could require a significant concession by the seller on its price—although exceptions have recently been made.[30] It is hard to draw a clear distinction, either in theory or in practice, between a premium to compensate an investor for market risk and a premium to compensate for liquidity risk. In fact, some analysts view the liquidity premium as a component of the market risk premium rather than as an addition to it because investors place a high value on liquidity during times of market stress, when a lack of liquidity can be costly. In general, attempts by researchers to identify a separate liquidity premium have produced inconsistent results. CBO did not attempt such a decomposition; its measure of the risk premium includes any liquidity premium. In addition, CBO did not adjust its results for any administrative costs in excess of the fees that were collected, because it expects such amounts to be relatively small.

A basic principle in valuing assets is that the cost of capital for a particular activity is based on the risk of the activity itself but is largely independent of how it is financed. Following that principle, the discount rates CBO used in calculating fair value subsidies reflect the risk associated with the assets under consideration, not the Federal Reserve's cost of borrowing. Borrowing costs are not in themselves a measure of the cost of capital for any specific activity but instead depend on the totality of the central bank's activities. Associating the cost of capital with the riskiness of the acquired assets is analogous to the way CBO estimates subsidies under the TARP: Such subsidies are based on the riskiness of the assets that the Treasury has acquired and not simply on its low cost of borrowing (stemming from the government's ability to raise taxes to cover the debt).

Considerable uncertainty surrounds CBO's estimates of fair value subsidies, which rely on assumptions about factors that are difficult to quantify, such as the probability, at the time the policies were implemented, that the crisis would deepen or abate, the amount that would be borrowed and the interest rates on that borrowing at such times, and the severity of any realized losses. The uncertainty associated with the estimates is asymmetric—that is, there is a high probability that the Federal Reserve will experience negligible losses or realize gains and a much smaller chance that it will experience significant losses. The possibility of such losses in part reflects the increase in borrowing that could occur under the Federal Reserve's riskier programs: For some of those programs, the central bank announced borrowing limits, but for others, no explicit limits were set.[31] As it turned out, in the months after those programs were introduced, the amounts lent by the riskiest facilities rose rapidly to total about $500 billion in December 2008. A few months later, however, such lending had begun a gradual decline as market conditions improved (see Figure 3).

For each of the Federal Reserve's stabilization programs, CBO reports the cost of fair value subsidies at the pro gram's inception date. Those estimates capture the full value of the Federal Reserve's commitments at the time they were made, taking into account all future cash flows over the life of the program and the uncertainty surrounding them. The Federal Reserve made significant— and in several cases repeated—changes to some of the programs as conditions in the markets changed. However, for this analysis, CBO based each set of its estimates on the information available at the time the program was created and did not adjust the estimates for subsequent changes that it could not have anticipated.

Subsidy Estimates

In CBO's estimation, the total amount of fair value subsidies conferred by the Federal Reserve's new emergency facilities at the time that the programs were created was about $21 billion (see Table 1 on page 8). Subsidy amounts varied considerably by program, but for the most part, they were modest. Several programs involving loans that were backed only by risky collateral, that had interest rates that were administratively set by the Federal Reserve, and that would extend over months or years gave rise to most of the subsidy costs. For other programs that were structured to pose very little risk to the central bank or that explicitly extended credit by using a competitive auction or a fair value basis, economic subsidies were judged to be negligible.

The Federal Reserve's emergency programs as well as the actions taken by the Treasury under the TARP involved subsidies conferred on financial institutions by the federal government. However, the total amount of subsidies provided by the Federal Reserve is much smaller than the subsidy arising from the TARP, which CBO estimated to be $189 billion at the program's inception. By design, the TARP encompassed a much greater assumption of risk by the government and some purchases of assets at prices significantly above their fair values.

Expanded Lending to Depository Institutions. In CBO's view, the expanded use of the Federal Reserve's discount window, lending by the Term Auction Facility, and, before 2009, the increased use of repurchase agreements did not create significant subsidies. The reciprocal currency arrangements (dollar swaps) that the central bank engaged in at various times throughout the crisis were struck at terms favorable to the Federal Reserve and thus had negative subsidies—they created profits for the government.

CBO judges the fair value subsidies conferred by the expanded use of the discount window and repurchase agreements to be negligible. That broader use is an extension of the Federal Reserve's normal lending activities, which are structured to minimize the risk of loss. The loans and agreements have short terms and are well collateralized; moreover, the loans from the discount window are recourse loans—that is, in case of default, the Federal Reserve has recourse to the assets of borrowers beyond the collateral that has been provided. On repurchase agreements, borrowers pay market rates of interest.

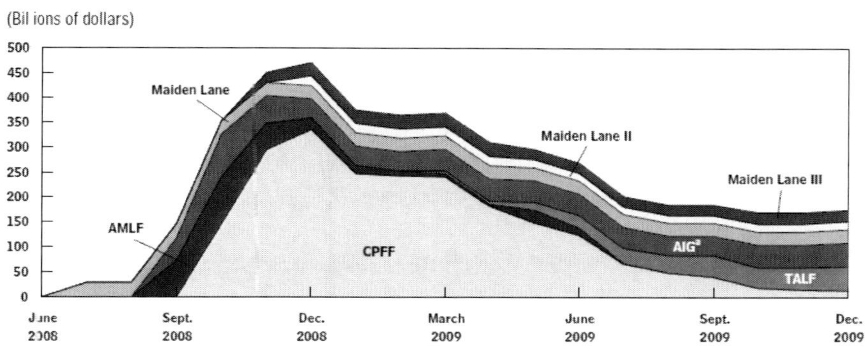

Source: Congressional Budget Office based on data from the Federal Reserve.

Notes: Further information on the programs can be found in Appendix A.

TALF = Term Asset-Backed Securities Loan Facility; AMLF = Asset-Backed Commercial Paper Money Market Mutual Fund Liquidity Facility; CPFF = Commercial Paper Funding Facility.

a. The data for the American International Group (AIG) comprise the outstanding balance on the line of credit plus equity holdings in AIA Aurora Limited Liability Company (LLC) and ALICO Holdings LLC.

Figure 3. Funding Provided Through Selected Federal Reserve Programs.

CBO has also concluded that the subsidies associated with the TAF are negligible. In principle, the longer maturity loans offered under the facility exposed the Federal Reserve to greater risk of loss than does its traditional overnight lending through the discount window. However, the TAF's requirements for large amounts of collateral up front to secure the loans made losses unlikely. Moreover, a TAF loan by design carried a market based interest rate because the rate was determined through a competitive auction (the minimum rate was 0.25 percent). Another reason to believe that the TAF offered little if any subsidy is that the facility's auctions were consistently undersubscribed after the height of the crisis, suggesting that many potential borrowers did not find the funds attractive even when they carried the minimum allowable rate under the facility.

The dollar swaps with foreign central banks have resulted in gains for the Federal Reserve. However, CBO did not have enough information about the terms on the swaps at the time the program was announced to estimate the prospective value of those commitments. As it turned out, the swaps exposed the Federal Reserve to very little risk of default because the other parties to the arrangements were foreign central banks, not the foreign private banks that borrowed the dollar denominated funds from their central banks. Nevertheless, the Federal Reserve received interest payments on the swaps that included compensation for the risk associated with the private foreign banks that ultimately borrowed the funds.[32] As a result, the interest rates charged on the swaps more than compensated the Federal Reserve for its risk exposure.

New Liquidity Programs for Nondepository Financial Institutions and Other Market Participants. The Federal Reserve created several programs to provide liquidity to nondepository institutions. Some of the facilities were designed to protect the central bank entirely from losses as a result of defaults or to compensate it at near market rates for the risks associated with such lending. But other facilities that the Federal Reserve established exposed it to risk that was not fully counterbalanced by higher interest rates or some other type of protection, such as collateral. In those cases, the Federal Reserve provided a subsidy to borrowers.

The Primary Dealer Credit Facility. With this facility, the Federal Reserve extended the use of its discount window to primary dealers—large financial institutions that are authorized to trade directly with the Federal Reserve System. As with traditional loans from the discount window, the Federal Reserve's risk of losses on loans to primary dealers was minimal because the loans were for short terms and were well collateralized; in addition, the Federal Reserve had recourse to the borrowers' assets in the event of their default. Hence, CBO estimates that the amount of the fair value subsidies provided on loans from this facility was negligible.

The Term Securities Lending Facility. The Federal Reserve created the Term Securities Lending Facility early in 2008 to strengthen the financing position of primary dealers and generally improve conditions in the financial markets. Through the facility, it lent Treasury securities to primary dealers for terms of 28 days; the loans were backed by dealers' pledged collateral of high grade securities. Dealers paid interest on the loaned securities at a rate determined in competitive auctions, and as a result, CBO has estimated that the loans were unsubsidized.

The Asset Backed Commercial Paper Money Market Mutual Fund Liquidity Facility and the Money Market Investor Funding Facility. The Federal Reserve created these pro grams to increase liquidity in the market for asset backed commercial paper and to assure investors that money market mutual funds would have sufficient liquidity to meet the elevated demand that the financial crisis might generate for the redemption of shares in the funds. (Large redemptions from money market funds are extremely rare except during periods of severe financial distress.) Under the terms of the AMLF, the Federal Reserve provided loans to depository institutions to purchase highly rated asset backed commercial paper from money market mutual funds at a fixed interest rate—the primary credit rate.[33] The commercial paper that was purchased served as collateral for the loan, and the Federal Reserve had no further recourse to the borrowers' assets in the event of default on the loan.

The MMIFF was a related facility that effectively supplemented the AMLF. CBO judged that the MMIFF would be used only in times of extreme distress; as a result, it estimated a negligible cost arising from the facility's activities. In fact, the MMIFF was never used and was dis continued on October 30, 2009.

Two factors suggest that the AMLF provided a subsidy to participants in the financial markets by charging a rate of interest that did not fully cover the riskiness of the collateral (the commercial paper) it was accepting on its loans. First, had the crisis worsened, the market value of the col lateral would probably have fallen below the principal owed on the loans, leaving the Federal Reserve exposed to losses. Second, although only highly rated commercial paper was eligible as collateral, credit ratings became less informative during the financial crisis, and money market mutual funds had an incentive to sell the AMLF their holdings of highly rated but relatively risky and illiquid paper, because there was no penalty for doing so.[34] CBO's estimates of fair value subsidies take into account the heightened level and volatility of commercial paper rates as well as the likelihood of additional borrowing from the facility in the event of a crisis (see Appendix B).

CBO estimates that at the inception of the AMLF, in September 2008, fair value subsidies totaled about $2 billion, reflecting the highly distressed market conditions prevailing at the time.

The Commercial Paper Funding Facility. The Federal Reserve designed the Commercial Paper Funding Facility, like the AMLF, to relieve stress in the money markets by increasing the liquidity of high quality commercial paper. The CPFF was a limited liability company authorized to buy highly rated, three month dollar denominated commercial paper (including asset backed commercial paper) using financing provided by the Federal Reserve. The commercial paper that it purchased served as collateral for that financing, and the Federal Reserve had recourse only to the assets of the facility.

The CPFF generated a subsidy because it provided participants in the financial markets with the option of borrowing money against risky collateral at terms that did not adjust with changes in conditions in the markets. The Federal Reserve charged an interest rate on loans through the CPFF that was high enough to discourage use of the facility under normal market conditions but that made its use attractive during times of extreme financial distress.[35] It is exactly at those times that the market value of the collateral for such loans would be at the greatest risk of falling short of the loans' principal, leaving the Federal Reserve at risk for losses. CBO's estimate of fair value subsidies for the CPFF takes into account the heightened level and volatility of rates during the crisis, but it also factors in the assumption that conditions will tend to revert to normal over time (see Appendix B).

CBO estimates that at the inception of the CPFF, in October 2008, the facility created a subsidy of about $2 billion. (At that point, the CPFF was scheduled to operate only until April 30, 2009, but the Federal Reserve later extended its operations to February 1, 2010. However, because CBO's analysis is intended to indicate the subsidy provided at the program's inception, the estimate does not take the cost of that extension into account.) As in the case of the other emergency facilities, the initial subsidy reflected conditions in the financial markets at that time.

The Term Asset Backed Securities Loan Facility. The financial crisis also caused a severe and protracted decline in the availability of financing for longer term asset backed securities. In November 2008, the Federal Reserve announced that it was creating the TALF to support segments of the asset backed securities market that provide a significant portion of the funding for certain types of commercial and consumer credit, such as commercial mortgages, auto loans, and credit cards. The facility was not actually opened until March 3, 2009, which CBO treats as the date of the program's inception.

The TALF exposes the Federal Reserve to the risk of losses from defaults because it provides multiyear funding against risky asset backed securities. At the inception of the program, the TALF offered three year loans; shortly thereafter, it extended the term to five years for loans against some types of collateral, such as securities backed by student loans or commercial mortgages. Loans from the TALF carry administratively set interest rates that differ for various types of qualifying collateral and loan maturities.

Despite the riskiness of the collateral backing the loans and their extended maturities (which leave lenders vulnerable to changes in economic conditions), three factors mitigate but do not eliminate the default risk that the Federal Reserve assumes when it makes such loans. First, the Treasury has provided the central bank with "first loss protection" on the loans, whereby the Treasury absorbs the first $20 billion of realized losses through the TARP. Second, the accumulated interest income on the TALF loans can be used to cover losses. Third, the Federal Reserve imposes "haircut" provisions that limit the amount of a loan to less than the full value of the collateral backing it. The riskier the class of assets backing the loan, the larger is the haircut that the central bank requires. CBO's estimate of the fair value subsidy from the TALF takes those three types of protection into account (see Appendix B).

In CBO's estimation, a subsidy of roughly $13 billion was generated at the inception of the TALF. Although the volume of lending under the program was initially small and increased only slowly, the subsidy that CBO calculated at the program's inception reflects the possibility that financial conditions might have worsened, leading to greater participation in the facility (as other alternatives became more expensive or unavailable) as well as losses that would have exceeded the amount of protection provided by the TARP.

Open-Market Purchases of Securities. Securities that the Federal Reserve purchases in the open market or in competitive auctions, in CBO's estimation, are acquired at prices that reflect their fair value. That reasoning applies to mortgage backed securities, agency debt, and Treasury securities. As such, no fair value subsidy is associated with those transactions.

Nevertheless, such transactions confer valuable benefits on participants in the financial markets that might be considered subsidies under a more comprehensive definition of the term. The Federal Reserve's purchases of securities boost the demand for them, thereby increasing their liquidity, pushing up their prices (and benefiting the securities' existing owners), and lowering their associated interest rates (which in the mortgage markets benefits home buyers).[36] However, the central bank's purchases also impose costs. For example, lower interest rates in general reduce the interest income of savers, whereas lower rates on mortgages increase the rate at which home owners prepay their mortgages, which diminishes the stream of income that owners of existing mortgage backed securities receive.

Support for Systemically Important Financial Institutions. Despite the serious financial problems that led the Federal Reserve to create facilities to support financial institutions it identified as systemically important—such as AIG and Citigroup—the central bank initially provided either no subsidy or only a small one to those institutions, in CBO's estimation. In the case of the Maiden Lane facilities, which were established to facilitate the Bear Stearns and AIG transactions, the Federal Reserve initially provided support on fair value terms. Its bolstering of Citigroup and Bank of America was structured so that the risk of losses was primarily borne by other federal entities, such as the Treasury (using funding from the TARP) and the FDIC.

The Maiden Lane Facilities. CBO estimates that no economic subsidies were associated with these facilities at their inception because the Federal Reserve reported that it had acquired portfolios of risky securities equal in fair value terms to the principal amounts of the loans that it extended. (In other words, there was an equal exchange of value.)

Line of Credit to the American International Group. The Federal Reserve initially extended an $85 billion line of credit to AIG to help it meet its obligations and restructure its operations with minimal disruption to the economy. CBO's estimate of the subsidy conferred at the inception of the program, when the line of credit was established, is about $2 billion. That estimate, however, is considerably more uncertain than estimates for the Federal Reserve's other programs because very little information was available about AIG's financial condition. A measure that is sometimes informative is the rates that other lenders offer on financing. However, in this case, such rates are not valid points of comparison because they take into account the government's backing, without which AIG would have failed. The Federal Reserve charged AIG very high interest rates on the loans, but the fact that AIG relied heavily on the line of credit and continues to draw on it suggests that the central bank's terms have continued to be more favorable than those available from private lenders.

Contingent Loans to Citigroup and Bank of America. The contingent loans to Citigroup and Bank of America initially provided small subsidies, in CBO's estimation. For the Citigroup portfolio, CBO estimated fair value subsidies of about $2 billion at the inception of the program. That amount is sensitive to assumptions about the size of the risk premium (among other factors), which CBO estimated to be 8 percent. If the risk premium was assumed to be 6 percent, then the subsidy at the inception of the program would be about $4 billion; if the risk premium was assumed to be 10 percent, then the subsidy would be about $8 billion.

The Federal Reserve was less exposed to losses from the Citigroup program than were the Treasury and the FDIC because those latter organizations had to absorb losses before the Federal Reserve suffered any. In addition, the central bank benefited from a relatively high rate of interest on the contingent loan—the three month overnight indexed swap rate plus 300 basis points—even though its risk was fairly limited.

On Bank of America's contingent loan, the subsidy that the Federal Reserve provided at the program's inception was less than $1 billion, in CBO's judgment.

APPENDIX A: PROGRAMS CREATED BY THE FEDERAL RESERVE DURING THE FINANCIAL CRISIS

During the past several years, the Federal Reserve significantly expanded the amount and availability of its lending to a broad range of financial institutions. It did so by invoking its authority under section 13(3) of the Federal Reserve Act of 1913 to lend "[i]n unusual and exigent circumstances" to "any individual, partnership, or corporation . . . unable to secure adequate credit accommodations from other banking institutions."[37]

Using that authority, the central bank expanded existing lending programs that provide liquidity to depository institutions, such as banks and credit unions, whose liabilities largely consist of checking and savings accounts and other deposits.[38] It also created new programs to provide liquidity to nondepository financial institutions and other market participants, such as brokers and dealers in securities and money market mutual funds; purchased mortgage related securities on the open market to try to help lower medium and long term interest rates and improve the flow of credit in the market for home mort gages; and extended direct loans and other support to certain "systemically important" financial institutions— those whose failures the central bank believed could lead to a systemic collapse of financial markets and institutions.

Table A-1. Overview of the Federal Reserve's Lending Programs during the Financial Crisis

	Participants	Collateral	Collateral "Haircuts"[a]	Loan Term	Interest Rates	Recourse[b]
Discount Window	Depository institutions	Full range of discount-window collateral (most loans that are not past due and most highly rated securities)	Haircuts for securities are between 1 percent and 18 percent of estimated fair market values; haircuts for loans are between 4 percent and 56 percent.	Typically overnight but up to 90 days during the financial crisis	Set as a spread over the target for the federal funds rate (the rate banks charge each other for overnight loans of their spare reserve balances)	Yes
Reciprocal Currency Arrangements	Selected central banks[c]	Foreign currency and eligible collateral in the central bank's jurisdiction	No	Overnight to 3 months	Equal to the rate earned by the foreign central banks on their loans to private banks	No
Term Auction Facility	Sound depository institutions	Full range of discount-window collateral (most loans that are not past due and most highly rated securities)	The same haircuts as for discount-window lending	Initially 28 days or 84 days	Set by auction. The minimum bid rate is the rate of interest that Federal Reserve Banks pay on excess reserve balances.	Yes
Primary Dealer Credit Facility	Primary dealers[d]	Full range of collateral accepted for triparty repurchase agreements (those in which a custodian bank or international clearing organization acts as an intermediary between the two parties to the agreement)	For collateral that is eligible for the Federal Reserve's open market operations (OMOs)—that is, Treasury securities, agency debt, and agency mortgage-backed securities—the haircuts are those used for OMOs. For non-OMO-eligible collateral, haircuts are based on the riskiness of the asset and are generally higher than for OMO-eligible collateral.	Overnight	Equal to the primary credit rate (the rate that sound banks pay on loans from the discount window) in effect at the Federal Reserve Bank of New York	Yes
Term Securities	Primary dealers[d]	Treasury securities, agency debt, and agency	For collateral that is eligible for the Federal Reserve's open	28 days	Set in an auction process subject to a minimum bid	No

	Participants	Collateral	Collateral "Haircuts"[a]	Loan Term	Interest Rates	Recourse[b]
Lending Facility		mortgage-backed securities, and all investment-grade debt securities	market operations (OMOs)—that is, Treasury securities, agency debt, and agency mortgage-backed securities—the haircuts are those used for OMOs. For non-OMO-eligible collateral, haircuts are based on the riskiness of the asset and are generally higher than for OMO-eligible collateral.		rate of 10 or 25 basis points, depending on the type of collateral used in the auction	
Asset-Backed Commercial Paper Money Market Mutual Fund Liquidity Facility	Depository institutions, bank holding companies, and U.S. branches and agencies of foreign banks	Highly rated asset-backed commercial paper	No	Maturity date of the asset-backed commercial paper but a 270-day maximum	Equal to the primary credit rate (the rate that sound banks pay on loans from the discount window) in effect at the Federal Reserve Bank of Boston at the time the advance is made	No
Money Market Investor Funding Facility	Eligible money market mutual funds and other money market investors	U.S. dollar-denominated certificates of deposit, bank notes, and commercial paper issued by highly rated financial institutions	No	Overnight	Equal to the primary credit rate (the rate that sound banks pay on loans from the discount window) in effect at the Federal Reserve Bank of New York	Yes
Funding Facility	Eligible issuers of commercial paper	Newly issued 3-month unsecured and asset-backed commercial paper from eligible U.S. issuers	No	3 months	The lending rate on asset-backed commercial paper is the 3-month overnight indexed swap (OIS) rate	Yes

Table A-1. (Continued)

	Participants	Collateral	Collateral "Haircuts"[a]	Loan Term	Interest Rates	Recourse[b]
					plus 300 basis points; for unsecured commercial paper, the rate is the 3-month OIS rate plus 100 basis points and an unsecured-credit surcharge of 100 basis points.	
Term Asset-Backed Securities Loan Facility	Investors in the United States who own eligible collateral	Recently originated U.S. dollar-denominated AAA-rated asset-backed securities and commercial mortgage-backed securities[e]	Haircuts vary from 5 percent to 16 percent, depending on the class of assets and a security's average life but not on the borrower.	3 or 5 years	Varies by the type of collateral securing the loan (and in some cases by the term of the loan)	No

Source: Congressional Budget Office.

Notes: See the text for further information on the programs in the table.

A basis point is one-hundredth of a percentage point.

a. The percentage of the collateral's value that cannot be used to back a loan.

b. In the event of a borrower's defaulting on a loan, the Federal Reserve has the right to collect the unpaid balance from the borrower.

c. European Central Bank, Bank of England, Swiss National Bank, Bank of Japan, Reserve Bank of Australia, Banco Central do Brasil, Bank of Canada, Danmarks Nationalbank, Bank of Korea, Bank of Mexico, Reserve Bank of New Zealand, Norway's Norges Bank, Monetary Authority of Singapore, and Sweden's Sveriges Riksbank.

d. Primary dealers are commercial banks and broker-dealers in securities that trade U.S. government and selected other securities with the Federal Reserve.

e. Underlying assets on the AAA-rated securities include auto loans, student loans, credit card loans, small business loans guaranteed by the Small Business Administration, mortgage-servicing advances, business equipment-related loans or leases, vehicle fleet leases, "floorplan" loans, and commercial mortgages.

Now that the turmoil in the financial markets has sub sided and most of the liquidity programs have ended, the Federal Reserve's holdings of mortgage related securities and its support of systemically important financial institutions remain on its balance sheet. (The lending programs are summarized in Table A1.)

Expanded Lending to Depository Institutions

The Federal Reserve's earliest actions to address the financial crisis, apart from the reduction in its target for the federal funds rate (the interest rate that banks charge each other for overnight loans of their spare reserve balances and that figures in the Federal Reserve's conduct of monetary policy), focused on providing liquidity to depository institutions.[39] The central bank eased the terms on which depository institutions could borrow from its so called discount window, increased its use of repurchase agreements to add liquidity to the banking system, expanded its currency swap lines with foreign central banks, and created the Term Auction Facility (TAF) to provide loans with longer terms through the discount window.

Expansion of Lending Through the Discount Window

The Federal Reserve extends credit directly to depository institutions through its discount window program, or facility. The discount window operates as a backup source of liquidity for individual depository institutions that are experiencing a temporary shortfall of reserves. The terms of loans from the window are very short, typically overnight, and the loans are backed by collateral. The interest rate on such loans—known as the discount rate—is usually set higher than the Federal Reserve's target for the federal funds rate.

Before the financial crisis, the total amount of borrowing from the discount window was small, for two main reasons: The Federal Reserve discouraged depository institutions from using the window as a regular source of funds, and a stigma attached to banks that borrowed from the window at a rate of interest that was higher than prevailing market rates (because such borrowing gave rise to suspicions that the banks might be in financial trouble).[40] Early in the crisis, the Federal Reserve sought to encourage borrowing from the window as a way of providing additional liquidity, and so it increased the term for borrowing to a maximum of 90 days and lessened the difference—known as the spread—between the discount rate and the federal funds rate.[41] The Federal Reserve extended the maturity on loans and lowered the cost of borrowing through the discount window several times during the crisis.

The outstanding amount of lending through the discount window (excluding lending for exceptional but predict able seasonal needs) spiked as the financial crisis unfolded, and it remained very high, by historical standards, at the end of 2009. Such credit increased from $3 million in July 2007 to $4.5 billion at the end of 2007; it peaked at almost $111 billion at the end of October 2008. The amount of outstanding loans from the discount window fell to about $49 billion by the end of June 2009 and to $20 billion by the end of last year.

Expanded Use of Repurchase Agreements

The Federal Reserve provided additional liquidity to depository institutions by increasing the amount of its repurchase agreements ("repos") with its primary dealers.[42] A repurchase agreement is similar to a collateralized loan. The Federal Reserve simultaneously agrees to buy a security and sell it back to the dealer on an agreed upon day—typically the following day but sometimes many days later. The difference between the price paid by the dealer to buy back the security and the price originally paid for it by the Federal Reserve is the interest that the primary dealer pays to the central bank for the term of the agreement. The interest rate depends on the riskiness of the collateral (that is, the security used in the agreement) and the creditworthiness of the borrower. Repurchase agreements increase reserves in the banking system until the dealer buys back the security because dealers deposit the proceeds of such sales in their banks.

In March 2008, to address strains in the markets for agency debt and agency guaranteed mortgage backed securities (MBSs), the Federal Reserve significantly increased its use of repurchase agreements by initiating the Single Tranche Open Market Operations Program.[43] The agreements had terms of 28 days, and the securities eligible for repurchase included agency debt and MBSs guaranteed by the agencies. Near the end of 2008, for example, agency MBSs made up 89 percent of the collateral for those agreements.[44]

The total amount of the repurchase agreements involving the Federal Reserve doubled to almost $110 billion after the Single Tranche Program began, and it remained high throughout the summer of 2008. As conditions in the financial markets improved, the Federal Reserve gradually reduced its repurchase transactions, and the amount outstanding reached zero in early 2009.

Extension of Reciprocal Currency Arrangements

In conjunction with other central banks, the Federal Reserve authorized reciprocal currency arrangements, also known as liquidity swap lines, to make available liquidity that was denominated in a foreign currency when it was temporarily needed. In the case of dollar swaps, the Federal Reserve makes a collateralized loan of U.S. dollars to a foreign central bank; because the responsibility to repay the loan rests with that bank, the credit risk that the Federal Reserve assumes (the risk that economic loss will result from the borrowers' failure to repay the loan) is exceedingly small.

Dollar Swap Lines. In December 2007, the Federal Reserve authorized the establishment of U.S. dollar swap lines to help the European Central Bank and the Swiss National Bank provide dollar denominated liquidity to foreign private banks in maturities ranging from overnight to three months. The foreign central banks obtained dollars to lend to institutions in their jurisdictions, and the Federal Reserve received assets denominated in euros and Swiss francs. Those arrangements initially provided dollars in amounts of up to $20 billion and $4 billion to the European Central Bank and the Swiss National Bank, respectively.[45] Because the demand for dollar funding continued to grow, the Federal Reserve set up swap lines with other central banks, and it increased the size and lengthened the terms of its existing lines with the European Central and Swiss National Banks. In the fall of 2008, the Federal Reserve eliminated the formal limits on the amounts of those lines as well as on the swap lines that had been set up with the Bank of Japan and the Bank of England, and it authorized new liquidity swap lines with 10 other central banks.[46] At the end of June 2009, the total amount of swaps outstanding was $119 billion, considerably less than the peak amount of $583 billion at the end of 2008. The Federal Reserve terminated those swap lines on February 1, 2010.

Foreign-Currency Swap Lines. In April 2009, the Federal Reserve announced that foreign currency swap lines had been set up with the Bank of England, the European Central Bank, the Bank of Japan, and the Swiss National Bank. Those liquidity lines were designed to give the Federal Reserve the capacity to provide U.S. financial institutions with liquidity denominated in foreign currencies. Through the swap lines, the Federal Reserve had access to sterling in amounts of up to £30 billion (approximately $44 billion at the time of the announcement), to euros in amounts of up to €80 billion (about $100 billion), to yen in amounts of up to ¥10 trillion (about $100 billion), and to Swiss francs in amounts of up to CHF40 billion (about $35 billion). The Federal Reserve did not draw on those lines, and they expired on February 1, 2010.

Establishment of the Term Auction Facility

The Federal Reserve created the Term Auction Facility in December 2007 as an extension of the discount win dow.[47] At two week intervals, the central bank initially auctioned a fixed amount of funds, secured by qualifying collateral, for terms of 28 or 84 days to depository institutions that were eligible to borrow under the primary credit program of the discount window.[48] The funds were not available to the borrowing institution immediately but were disbursed three days after the auction. Those features of the TAF meant that it was not suited to institutions that were experiencing a sudden need for liquidity, and thus borrowing from the TAF was less likely to raise concerns in the market about an institution's viability. As a result, depository institutions were expected to be more inclined to borrow through the TAF than through the normal discount window.

Indeed, term auction credit accounted for the majority of the Federal Reserve's lending to depository institutions during the crisis. At the peak of such lending, in early March 2009, loans through the TAF amounted to $493 billion, or almost 90 percent of total borrowing by depositories. By mid-2009, as the strains in the financial markets eased, banks' use of the TAF fell off sharply, and loans by the facility amounted to $283 billion. Consequently, the central bank has reduced the amount and maturity of the credit available at the auctions.[49] By the end of 2009, the amount of TAF loans had dropped to $76 billion.

New Programs for Nondepository Financial Institutions and Other Market Participants

As the financial crisis deepened, the Federal Reserve created new programs to provide liquidity directly to other financial institutions and market participants—in particular, primary dealers, money market mutual funds, and participants in the markets for commercial paper and asset backed securities.

The Primary Dealer Credit Facility

Exercising its emergency authority in March 2008, the Federal Reserve extended the privilege of discount window borrowing to primary dealers through its new Primary Dealer Credit Facility (PDCF). Many dealers faced difficulties in financing their holdings of mortgage backed and other securities. In more normal circumstances, they would have funded a significant portion of those holdings through repurchase agreements, with more than half of the contracts having overnight maturities.[50] But the prices of securities backed by subprime and other risky mortgages (loans made to borrowers with poorer than average credit) fell as losses on the under lying loans mounted, and the dealers had trouble finding counterparties (the legal and financial term for the other parties to the dealers' contracts) who would accept those securities as collateral for repurchase agreements. Many dealers faced the prospect of selling some of their securities at a substantial loss, which would have put further downward pressure on prices and possibly threatened some dealers with insolvency.

The amount of borrowing under the PDCF fluctuated markedly in 2008 but wound down to zero in 2009. By March 26, 2008, less than two weeks after the facility's creation, borrowings had climbed to more than $37 billion. The outstanding amount of loans from the PDCF began to fall steadily after that, and by the beginning of July, the facility was little used. When the turmoil in the financial markets intensified in September 2008, the PDCF's balance soared from zero to almost $147 billion on October 1. Since then, the need for the facility has diminished, and by the end of May 2009, lending by the PDCF had halted. The Federal Reserve terminated the facility on February 1, 2010.

The Term Securities Lending Facility

The Federal Reserve created the Term Securities Lending Facility (TSLF) in March 2008 to strengthen the financing position of primary dealers and, more generally, to foster improved conditions in the financial markets.[51] Through the TSLF, the Federal Reserve loaned U.S. Treasury securities to primary dealers in two types of auctions that differed by the collateral that dealers could offer in exchange for the loans.[52] The Federal Reserve made available up to $200 billion of Treasury securities to lend to primary dealers for terms of 28 days.

In July 2008, the Federal Reserve created the TSLF Options Program to auction options to obtain shorter term TSLF loans on future dates. The options program was intended to enhance the effectiveness of the TSLF by offering liquidity during periods when the demand for short term funds was high, such as at the end of a quarter.

By the last quarter of 2008, the amount of borrowing under the TSLF was close to the maximum. However, as conditions in the markets improved, borrowing diminished until outstanding loans totaled $27 billion at the end of May 2009. Consequently, in June of that year, the Federal Reserve announced that it was scaling back the program, and activity had ceased by the end of August. The facility expired on February 1, 2010.

The Asset-Backed Commercial Paper Money Market Mutual Fund Liquidity Facility

Money market mutual funds typically invest in short term debt, such as Treasury bills, certificates of deposit, and commercial paper (unsecured short term promissory notes issued primarily by corporations).[53] With those investments, money market funds provide a significant amount of financing for the asset backed commercial paper market, on which some financial institutions depend for short term loans. Unexpected losses at one such fund as a result of the bankruptcy of the Lehman Brothers investment bank in the fall of 2008 triggered a run by the fund's investors. That brought about a loss of confidence in the safety of money market funds more generally and led many investors to redeem their shares.

The Federal Reserve created the Asset Backed Commercial Paper Money Market Mutual Fund Liquidity Facility (AMLF) on September 19, 2008, to help money market funds meet spikes in the demand for redemptions and to foster confidence in the markets for asset backed commercial paper and in the broader money markets.[54] The AMLF provided funding to depository institutions and bank holding companies to finance their purchases of high quality asset backed commercial paper from money market funds under certain conditions.[55]

Lending through the AMLF began the week of September 22, 2008; by the beginning of October, the facility's balance had shot up to $152 billion. The balance steadily declined to less than $1 billion in April 2009, but it temporarily rose to almost $29 billion in early May and then fell to less than $16 billion at the end of June 2009.[56] With liquidity in the money markets improving significantly, the Federal Reserve announced in June 2009 that it would restrict participation in the AMLF to money market mutual funds that were experiencing "material" withdrawals of funds. The program expired on February 1, 2010.

The Money Market Investor Funding Facility

To ensure that money market funds had sufficient backup liquidity to pay investors in the event of a run, the Federal Reserve created the Money Market Investor Funding Facility in October 2008. The program was initially structured to provide financing to five special purpose vehicles (SPVs). SPVs are legal entities that are created to serve a particular function; the SPVs in this case were authorized to purchase dollar denominated certificates of deposit, bank notes, and commercial paper from eligible participants in the money markets.[57] (The commercial paper that the SPVs bought had to be issued by highly rated financial institutions and have remaining maturities of at least 7 days and no more than 90 days.) The Federal Reserve set the maximum amount of purchases by all of the SPVs at $600 billion. However, the backup facility was never used, and its authority expired on October 30, 2009.

The Commercial Paper Funding Facility

The market for commercial paper is an important source of short term funding for financial institutions and for some commercial firms. In the fall of 2008, the commercial paper market was under considerable strain—which was exacerbated by the bankruptcy of Lehman Brothers—because money market mutual funds and other investors that needed liquidity became increasingly reluctant to purchase commercial paper, especially at maturities that extended beyond overnight. As a result, the volume of outstanding commercial paper diminished, interest rates on longer term commercial paper rose significantly, and an increasingly large percentage of outstanding paper had to be refinanced each day.[58]

The Federal Reserve created the Commercial Paper Funding Facility (CPFF) in October 2008 to address the difficulties in the commercial paper market. The facility bought highly rated, three month dollar denominated commercial paper (including asset backed commercial paper) using financing provided by the Federal Reserve. The central bank set the borrowing terms so as to dis courage the use of the facility except when the spreads between the interest rates on commercial paper and those on relatively risk free securities (in general, Treasury securities) reached abnormally high levels. The interest rate on the paper was set at the three month overnight indexed swap rate plus 1 percentage point for unsecured paper and 3 percentage points for asset backed paper.[59] A surcharge of 1 percentage point was also levied on unsecured paper, and each issuer was required to pay a fee to the facility equal to 10 basis points (a basis point is one hundredth of a percentage point) of the maximum amount of the issuer's commercial paper that the CPFF might own.[60]

Use of the facility increased rapidly. By the end of 2008, net holdings in the CPFF's portfolio amounted to $334 billion. By the end of June 2009, the facility's holdings had fallen to $124 billion. Some of that decline, according to the Federal Reserve, can be traced to the lack of renewal of a significant portion of the maturing issues, possibly because improvements in overall market conditions may have allowed some borrowers to secure funding from other sources.[61] By the end of 2009, the facility held $14 billion in loans. Like many of the other lending facilities that the Federal Reserve created during the crisis, the CPFF expired on February 1, 2010.

The Term Asset-Backed Securities Loan Facility

In addition to its effects on short term financing, the financial crisis caused a severe decline in the availability of financing for longer term asset backed securities. In November 2008, the Federal Reserve created the Term Asset Backed Securities Loan Facility (TALF) to support segments of the market for asset backed securities that provide a significant portion of the funding for certain types of commercial and consumer credit. Under the program, the Federal Reserve was prepared to lend up to $200 billion to holders of certain AAA rated asset backed securities (that is, those assigned the highest possible commercial rating and hence the least risk of default) whose underlying assets consisted of recently originated qualifying loans.[62] (Included were auto loans, student loans, credit card loans, equipment loans, "floorplan" loans, insurance premium finance loans, loans guaranteed by the Small Business Administration, and residential mortgage servicing advance receivables.)[63] Also eligible as collateral were certain high quality commercial mortgage backed securities issued before January 1, 2009. Loans from the TALF are limited to terms of three or five years and carry administratively set interest rates that differ for various types of qualifying collateral and loan maturities.[64]

Lending under the TALF has gradually increased since the facility began operating in March 2009, rising from less than $5 billion during that month to more than $25 billion at the end of June and almost $48 billion at the end of the year. Unless the Federal Reserve extends the deadlines, the TALF is scheduled to stop making loans against newly issued commercial mortgage backed securities on June 30, 2010; it stopped making loans against all other collateral on March 31, 2010.

Open-Market Purchases of Securities

The Federal Reserve began purchasing securities in late 2008 in an effort to lower medium and long term interest rates, including mortgage rates, and thereby support the housing market and the broader economy. Fannie Mae and Freddie Mac—the two government sponsored enterprises that together accounted for about one half of the outstanding amount of home mortgages—had had trouble raising funds as their losses mounted in 2008, and their difficulties continued after they were put into conservatorship (placed under government control) by their regulator, the Federal Housing Finance Agency, in September 2008.[65] In addition, the demand for mortgage backed securities guaranteed by the two companies fell as investors worried about the companies' ability to honor their guarantees on the MBSs. Consequently, the Federal Reserve began purchasing the securities (agency debt) issued by Fannie Mae, Freddie Mac, and the Federal Home Loan Banks as well as mortgage-backed securities guaranteed by Fannie Mae, Freddie Mac, and Ginnie Mae (agency MBSs).[66] The central bank also purchased long term Treasury securities in 2009.

Agency Debt

The Federal Reserve began purchasing the debt of Fannie Mae, Freddie Mac, and the Federal Home Loan Banks at auction in September 2008. At first, it purchased only short term debt, with maturities of one year or less. Then, in November of that year, the central bank announced that it would acquire up to $100 billion in agency debt, and it began purchasing debt with longer terms in December. In March 2009, the central bank announced that it had increased to $200 billion the maximum amount of agency debt that it would purchase, but in early November, it stated that it would instead purchase a total of about $175 billion by the end of March 2010. By the end of 2009, it had purchased almost $160 billion in agency debt.

Agency Mortgage-Backed Securities

Initially, the Federal Reserve announced plans to buy up to $500 billion in agency MBSs, and it began making those purchases in mid-January 2009. In March, the central bank raised the planned amount of purchases to $1,250 billion. At the beginning of July 2009, the Federal Reserve owned $462 billion in those securities. At the end of 2009, it owned $908 billion.

Medium- and Long-Term Treasury Securities

At the end of July 2007, before the financial crisis began, the Federal Reserve owned $514 billion in Treasury notes and bonds.[67] That amount had fallen to $457 billion by mid-2008. In March 2009, the Federal Reserve announced its intention to purchase up to $300 billion in notes and bonds over the following six months. By the end of October of that year, the central bank had completed those purchases, bringing the amount of its holdings of notes and bonds to just over $756 billion.

Support for Systemically Important Financial Institutions

In conjunction with the Treasury and the Federal Deposit Insurance Corporation (FDIC), the Federal Reserve has provided substantial additional support to four institutions whose financial problems were believed to seriously threaten the stability of the financial system. That support included lending to the first Maiden Lane facility (related to the sale of the investment bank Bear Stearns), a line of credit to the American International Group (AIG), lending to the Maiden Lane II and Maiden Lane III facilities (which own certain assets formerly owned by AIG), and so called contingent lines of credit (components of the asset guarantees, which can be drawn on as needed) to Citigroup and Bank of America.

Lending Related to the Sale of the Bear Stearns Companies

In mid-March 2008, the large investment bank Bear Stearns informed the Federal Reserve, the Treasury, and the Securities and Exchange Commission that it might soon be unable to roll over (or refinance) its liabilities related to repurchase agreements. That possibility raised the concern that the sudden failure of Bear Stearns might have a chaotic effect on key financial markets, creating turmoil that could have severely undermined confidence and cast doubt on the financial stability of other major financial firms.

To prevent the adverse economic consequences that could have been triggered by a disorderly failure of Bear Stearns, the Federal Reserve, in consultation with the Treasury, agreed to extend funding to Bear Stearns through JPMorgan Chase & Company, to provide some time to resolve Bear Stearns' problems.[68] JPMorgan Chase subsequently agreed to purchase Bear Stearns and assume its financial obligations; the acquisition was completed on June 26, 2008. However, JPMorgan Chase did not acquire all of the nearly $400 billion in assets in Bear Stearns' portfolio. As part of the agreement, mortgage related assets from Bear Stearns valued at approximately $30 billion were segregated into a newly formed limited liability company (LLC) called Maiden Lane.[69] Maiden Lane's assets were financed by loans of nearly $29 billion from the Federal Reserve Bank of New York and $1 billion from JPMorgan Chase, with JPMorgan Chase liable for the first $1 billion of any losses sustained by Maiden Lane. (The overall portfolio is managed and will be liquidated by BlackRock, an investment management firm retained by the Federal Reserve Bank of New York.)

That arrangement is a significant shift from the Federal Reserve's usual policy of extending loans that not only have recourse provisions—in the event of default, the central bank has recourse to the assets of borrowers beyond the collateral provided—but also protection through collateral requirements. Although the financing takes the form of a loan from the Federal Reserve Bank of New York to Maiden Lane, the Federal Reserve essentially has acquired the underlying assets—that is, it has taken on all of the risk of those assets (with the exception of the $1 billion from JPMorgan Chase) and has control of the Maiden Lane facility.

Support to American International Group

AIG, a large and diversified financial institution, experienced serious financial problems in September 2008 stemming from one of its subsidiaries' involvement in the market for subprime residential mortgage loans. AIG suffered large losses on its investments in securities backed by subprime mortgages and on the credit default swaps— essentially insurance policies—it sold on such securities.[70] AIG faced a crisis as its lenders, worried about its capacity to meet its debts, refused to continue to provide financing. With slightly more than $1 trillion in consolidated assets at the end of September 2008, AIG was an important firm with dealings around the world. Its collapse would have created problems for its counterparties and for other financial institutions at a time when the financial markets had been badly shaken by the failure of Lehman Brothers a few days earlier.

The assistance that the Federal Reserve provided to AIG was channeled through four distinct facilities: a line of credit, the Securities Borrowing Facility, Maiden Lane II, and Maiden Lane III.

The line of credit to AIG is a facility that has been modified significantly since it was initiated on September 16, 2008. At that time, the Federal Reserve agreed to lend AIG up to $85 billion to help it meet its obligations and sell some of its businesses with the least possible disruption to the overall economy. As part of the arrangement, the U.S. government received warrants (a warrant pro vides the option but not the obligation to purchase stock at a fixed price) for a 79.9 percent ownership stake in AIG and the right to veto the payment of dividends to common and preferred shareholders. On October 8, following the revelation of additional problems at AIG, the Federal Reserve announced the creation of the Securities Borrowing Facility, under which it would lend up to about $38 billion against investment grade debt securities held by AIG. ("Investment grade" is a rating that indicates that a municipal or corporate bond has a relatively low risk of default.)

In November 2008, the arrangement with AIG was again modified to provide additional federal support. The Treasury announced that it would purchase $40 billion of newly issued AIG preferred shares under the TARP, which allowed the Federal Reserve to reduce the total amount available under the line of credit from $85 billion to $60 billion. The central bank also lengthened the maximum term of its loans under the line of credit to five years and lowered the interest rate on the outstanding balances as well as the fee charged on the unused portion of the credit line.[71]

In November as well, the Federal Reserve announced plans to restructure its lending related to AIG by extending credit to two newly formed limited liability companies:

- The first, Maiden Lane II LLC, received a loan of $22.5 billion from the Federal Reserve and a subordinated loan—a loan that is repaid after the loan from the Federal Reserve—of $1 billion from AIG, with which Maiden Lane purchased residential mortgage backed securities from AIG. As a result of those actions, the Securities Borrowing Facility established on October 8 was subsequently repaid and terminated.
- The second new company, Maiden Lane III LLC, received a loan of $30 billion from the Federal Reserve and a subordinated loan of $5 billion from AIG. With those funds, it purchased certain securities as part of an arrangement to terminate related credit default swap contracts that AIG had written.

Under Maiden Lane II and Maiden Lane III, the Federal Reserve essentially acquired mortgage backed securities at prices judged to represent fair values—that is, the prices that would be received by selling the assets in orderly transactions between market participants. Ultimately, the central bank will realize gains or losses on those securities, depending on the underlying loans' performance over time.

In June 2009, the Federal Reserve agreed to reduce the line of credit to AIG by $25 billion in exchange for preferred shares in two of AIG's largest life insurance units outside of the United States: American International Assurance and American Life Insurance Company. That transaction was completed in December 2009.

The assistance to AIG from federal sources totaled approximately $128 billion outstanding at the end of 2009. Of that amount, $81 billion had been provided by the Federal Reserve, and $47 billion had come from the TARP.

Contingent Loan to Citigroup

The financial condition of Citigroup, the largest commercial bank in the United States at the beginning of 2008, deteriorated near the end of that year, raising questions about the bank's solvency. On November 23, 2008, the Treasury and the FDIC arranged a guarantee (against losses) on $301 billion of Citigroup's assets, more than half of which were residential and commercial real estate loans. The guarantee on the bank's residential assets was to last for 10 years; the guarantee on its nonresidential assets was for 5 years. Under that arrangement, the first $39.5 billion in losses would be absorbed by Citigroup. Additional losses (subject to loss sharing of 10 percent by Citigroup) would be absorbed first by the Treasury (up to $5 billion), then by the FDIC (up to $10 billion), and finally by the Federal Reserve (the remainder). In the event that losses exceeded the resources pledged by Citi group, the Treasury, and the FDIC, the Federal Reserve would be obligated to issue a nonrecourse loan to Citi group, backed by the remaining assets, with an interest rate tied to an overnight borrowing rate plus 3 percentage points. Effectively, if that contingency had arisen, the assets would have been sold to the central bank at their current values.

In December 2009, Citigroup terminated its agreement with the Treasury, the Federal Deposit Insurance Corporation, and the Federal Reserve and paid an exit fee of $50 million to the central bank. The Federal Reserve experienced no losses on this guarantee because Citigroup never used the line of credit.

Contingent Loan to Bank of America

Bank of America experienced intense borrowing problems early in 2009, when it announced losses on its business operations in the fourth quarter of 2008. The Treasury and the FDIC agreed to guarantee $118 billion of the bank's assets under terms similar to those extended to Citigroup. The guarantee on the bank's residential assets was to last 10 years; the guarantee on its nonresidential assets was for 5 years. Under the guarantee agreement, the first $10 billion in losses would be absorbed by Bank of America. Additional losses (subject to loss sharing of 10 percent by the bank) would be absorbed by the Treasury (up to $7.5 billion) and the FDIC (up to $2.5

billion). If the backing to be provided by those two entities was exhausted, the Federal Reserve would be obligated to lend Bank of America up to a maximum of $87.2 billion with the bank's remaining assets as collateral. Bank of America did not request activation of the guarantee and in September 2009 paid an exit fee of $57 million to the Federal Reserve to terminate the arrangement.

APPENDIX B: CBO'S FAIR-VALUE MODELS

Some of the Federal Reserve's programs to provide credit to financial institutions during the financial crisis offered terms that were more favorable than the terms those borrowers could have obtained from private investors—thereby providing fair value subsidies on that credit. To estimate such subsidies, the Congressional Budget Office (CBO) developed a stochastic simulation model for each major program. In general, under that approach, CBO projected probability distributions of future cash flows associated with each program and then discounted the cash flows to their present value using rates that reflected the risk associated with the particular flows.[72] The probability distribution of a program's cash flows depended on several factors: the program's rules and structure; the probability distributions of interest rates, default rates, and recovery rates on defaults; and how the demand for a program was affected by those variables.

CBO used such models to estimate the fair value subsidies provided by the Asset Backed Commercial Paper Money Market Mutual Fund Liquidity Facility (AMLF), the Commercial Paper Funding Facility (CPFF), and the Term Asset Backed Securities Loan Facility (TALF). CBO also used a similar approach to evaluate the subsidies provided by the contingent loan programs that the Federal Reserve extended to Citigroup and Bank of America. (For additional information on the programs, see Appendix A.)

The Asset-Backed Commercial Paper Money Market Mutual Fund Liquidity Facility

CBO's estimate of the subsidies provided by the AMLF is based on a model of the probability distribution of future spreads, or differences, between the interest rates on three month AA rated asset backed commercial paper and the primary credit rate and a rule for when and how much depositories will borrow to fund their commercial paper purchases. The model uses historical data on those spreads, which are a measure of stress in the market for commercial paper. In addition, the model accounts for the heightened level and volatility of commercial paper rates during a crisis.

In the model, new borrowing through the facility occurs when the spread rises above its long run level by two or more standard deviations. At such a time, some money market funds may experience a surge in the demand for redemptions that could result in new borrowing under the facility. CBO assumed that new borrowing would equal, on average, 2 percent of outstanding balances in U.S. money market mutual funds. It also assumed that the new loans and their underlying collateral would have average maturities of 90 days and that once the loans matured, additional borrowing would not occur unless crisis conditions continued or reemerged.[73]

CBO calculated the monthly value of the subsidies provided by the facility in two steps. First, it multiplied the facility's outstanding balances by 1 percent or the spread between the commercial paper and the primary credit rate, whichever was larger. It then discounted those monthly values back to September 2008, the date of the program's inception. The subsidies are based on averages calculated from more than 5,000 stochastic simulations.

The Commercial Paper Funding Facility

CBO's estimate of the subsidies provided through the CPFF, like its estimate for the AMLF, is based on a stochastic model of commercial paper spreads and a rule for when and how much commercial paper will be sold to this facility. CBO calibrated the model of commercial paper spreads by using historical data, taking into account the heightened level and volatility of rates during the crisis.

CBO assumed that new borrowing under the facility would occur only when rate spreads increased above their average precrisis level by two or more standard deviations. It also assumed that the amount of the facility's new borrowing would respond to interest rate conditions similarly to the way such borrowing responded in the early months of the program.

CBO calculated the monthly subsidy value by multiplying the facility's outstanding balances by the maximum of 1 percent or the difference between an interest rate on three month AA rated commercial paper (calculated as one third of the rate on financial paper plus two thirds of the rate on asset backed paper) and the rate charged to borrowers under the facility by the Federal Reserve.[74] It then discounted those monthly values back to October 2008, when the program was created. CBO's estimates are based on averages calculated over 5,000 simulations of the stochastic model.

The Term Asset-Backed Securities Loan Facility

CBO's approach to estimating the economic subsidy created by the Federal Reserve's activities through the TALF is based on several factors:

- The type of securities that serve as collateral and the risk associated with them;
- The effect of protection against losses provided by the Troubled Asset Relief Program (TARP) and the Federal Reserve's "haircut" provisions, which restrict the amount of a loan to less than the value of the posted collateral;
- The prevailing market rates for loans backed by similar collateral; and
- The projected volume of future lending, which is based on CBO's 10 year (2011 to 2020) baseline bud get projections for the program.

In estimating subsidies generated by the TALF's activities, CBO used market rates to calibrate a stochastic pricing model for each type of asset backed security that was used as collateral for a loan; it then used the model to estimate the fair value of the TALF's cash flows to the Federal Reserve, taking into account the protection against losses that various features of the facility afforded. The amount of protection offered by the Treasury was uncertain. It was initially set at $20 billion and was not explicitly raised when the Federal Reserve announced that it would consider expanding the size of the facility from $200 billion to $1 trillion. In calculating subsidies, CBO considered it likely that additional TARP protection would have been advanced had the volume of borrowing or the amounts of losses increased, and thus it assumed that the TARP would also cover 70 percent of any losses by the TALF in excess of the $20 billion that was explicitly provided. CBO based its subsidy calculations on projections of the amount of TALF lending that would be outstanding over time—CBO assumed $40 billion in new activity each month over the life of the facility.

Contingent Loans to Citigroup and Bank of America

The Federal Reserve offered Citigroup and Bank of America contingent loans that provided the banks with the option of drawing funds at a future date at a preset interest rate, with the funds to be secured only by risky collateral. Those contracts gave the banks a valuable funding alternative but one that they would be likely to use only if the terms were more attractive than what was available in the open market. To the extent that the fair value of the option exceeded the value of the fees and the interest that the Federal Reserve could expect to receive, the option provided a fair value subsidy to the banks.

CBO calculated the subsidy using a stochastic model of the Federal Reserve's expected cash flows under those arrangements. The model used projected future interest payments, repayments of principal, losses from default, and the value of the collateral assets.[75] CBO assumed, on the basis of the riskiness of the various classes of assets that could serve as collateral, that at the time the contingent loans were set up, the fair value of that collateral was significantly less than the amount that could be borrowed.

End Notes

[1] When the market for a financial asset is liquid, the asset can be readily and inexpensively converted to cash at a price that will not be very different from the price of the previous transaction. (Financial assets are claims that entitle the owner to receive a payment or a series of payments from an entity to which the owner has provided funds. They include bank accounts, retirement accounts, stocks and bonds, and various kinds of securities.) When markets become illiquid, large quantities of the asset cannot be sold (or bought) without at least temporarily depressing (or raising) the asset's price. The Federal Reserve can increase liquidity in a market—essentially make it easier to convert assets to cash— by standing ready to buy securities or to lend against them as collateral.

[2] Net lending is negative when the amount of repayments and losses on all types of lending exceeds the amount of new lending.

[3] A depository institution's reserve requirement is based on the type and amount of its deposits. Historically, most banks have held small amounts of excess reserves because reserves did not earn interest. However, the Emergency Economic Stabilization Act of 2008 (Division A of Public Law 110-343) authorized the Federal Reserve, as of October 1, 2008, to begin paying interest on reserves.

[4] When the Federal Reserve makes a loan to a bank, for example, it credits the reserve balances of the bank by the amount of the loan, thereby increasing both its assets (its lending to banks) and its liabilities (reserve balances held at the Federal Reserve) by the same amount. For more information on the relationship between the Federal Reserve's activities during the financial crisis and bank reserves, see Todd Keister and James J. McAndrews, "Why Are Banks Holding So Many Excess Reserves?" *Current Issues in Economics and Finance*, Federal Reserve Bank of New York, vol. 15, no. 8 (December 2009), available at www.newyorkfed.org/ research/current_issues/ci15 8.pdf.

[5] Congressional Budget Office, *An Analysis of the President's Budget ary Proposals for Fiscal Year 2011* (March 2010).

[6] As such, a fair value reflects the presence of a risk premium, which is the additional rate of return that investors require to bear market risk—the risk that losses will be greatest during times of economic stress. See Financial Accounting Standards Board, *Statement of Financial Accounting Standards No. 157, Fair Value Measurements* (September 2006), p. 2.

[7] The discounted value of a future stream of promised cash flows is the amount they are worth today—their present value. The dis counted value is calculated by applying a "discount rate" to future cash flows that accounts for the time value of money and for the risk of the cash flows.

[8] The measure is described in Congressional Budget Office, *The Troubled Asset Relief Program: Report on Transactions Through December 31, 2008* (January 2009).

[9] For the Federal Credit Reform Act of 1990, see title XIII, section 13201, of the Omnibus Budget Reconciliation Act of 1990; 2 U.S.C. 661, 104 Stat. 1388 610. The law specifies that in calculating those subsidy costs, interest rates on Treasury securities with similar maturities be used as discount rates (to determine the present value of the expected cash flows associated with a loan or loan guarantee). Because Treasury securities are considered to have little chance of default, their interest rates do not include a charge for the cost of default risk.

[10] CBO's estimates of the fair value subsidies provided by the TARP at or near the inception date of that program are described in Congressional Budget Office, *The Troubled Asset Relief Program: Report on Transactions Through December 31, 2008*. By design, some activities pursued under the TARP involved a much greater assumption of risk by the government and the purchase of some assets at prices that were significantly above their fair values. CBO now estimates that the TARP will cost $109 billion.

[11] A currency swap line is an arrangement between the Federal Reserve and a foreign central bank to temporarily trade an amount of U.S. dollars for an equivalent amount of a foreign currency.

[12] Primary dealers—commercial banks as well as brokers and dealers who buy and sell U.S. government and other securities in the private financial markets—trade with the Federal Reserve. Such firms must meet requirements set by the central bank for liquidity and capital as well as for other aspects of their operations. The market for commercial paper (unsecured short term promissory notes issued primarily by corporations) is an important source of funding for financial institutions and some commercial firms. Asset backed securities derive their income from the assets—for example, a pool of credit card loans—that back the securities.

[13] Money market mutual funds are a significant source of short term funding for financial institutions as well as for some corporations and government entities. For investors, the funds are an alternative to bank deposits: They pay a slightly higher rate of interest, but they expose investors to greater risk because they are not insured.

[14] Fannie Mae and Freddie Mac (formally, the Federal National Mortgage Association and the Federal Home Loan Mortgage Corporation) are two federally chartered institutions that provide credit guarantees for almost half of the outstanding residential mortgages in the United States. After the two firms experienced sizable losses on their mortgage related investments and guarantees, the Treasury placed them in conservatorship—essentially the government took control of them—in September 2008. Ginnie Mae is a government owned corporation that guarantees securities backed by federally insured loans—mainly loans insured by the Federal Housing Administration and the Department of Veterans Affairs. The Federal Home Loan Banks are government sponsored enterprises that lending institutions use to obtain low cost financing through "advances," which are loans backed by high quality collateral.

[15] In a limited liability company, the profits and losses of the business pass through to its owners, although, as the name implies, this particular legal structure offers protection from personal liability for business debts, just as a corporation does.

[16] The Federal Reserve also created the Securities Borrowing Facility to help AIG avoid selling a portfolio of residential mortgage backed securities in a weak market, but the facility was terminated about two months later upon the creation of Maiden Lane II. See Board of Governors of the Federal Reserve System, *Report Pursuant to Section 129 of the Emergency Economic Stabilization Act of 2008: Securities Borrowing Facility for American International Group, Inc.*, available at www.federalreserve.gov/monetarypolicy/files/129aigsecborrowfacility.pdf.

[17] The contingent loan to the Bank of America was in the form of a line of credit, which was never opened.

[18] The Federal Reserve's expenses include those for its operations (mostly salaries and employee benefits) and various interest payments, such as interest on reserves (see Box 1 on page 2).

[19] Congressional Budget Office, *The Budget and Economic Outlook: Fiscal Years 2010 to 2020* (January 2010), pp. 91–92.

[20] The accounting treatment of the assets held by the Maiden Lane facilities differs from the treatment of the Federal Reserve's other assets, most of which are valued at their historical cost. As a result, earnings on those assets are based on realized gains and losses rather than on changes in the assets' estimated fair values.

[21] If such losses occurred and caused the Federal Reserve's net earnings to become negative, the central bank would have no income to remit to the Treasury. In that case, the Treasury would not be obligated to make payments to the Federal Reserve to cover the losses.

[22] See Chapter 2 in Congressional Budget Office, *The Budget and Economic Outlook: Fiscal Years 2010 to 2020.*

[23] That estimate incorporates the assumption that the facilities remain on the central bank's balance sheet until they are completely wound down. However, the Treasury has announced its intention to assume financial responsibility for the Maiden Lane facilities "[i]n the longer term and as its authorities permit." See *The Role of the Federal Reserve in Preserving Financial and Monetary Stability: Joint Statement by the Department of the Treasury and the Federal Reserve* (March 23, 2009), available at www.treas.gov/ press/releases/tg66.htm. Such action would not change the financial position of the federal government.

[24] Of that $3.7 billion loss, $3.1 billion is attributable to the initial Maiden Lane company and $600 million to Maiden Lane II. The central bank has suffered no losses on its investment in Maiden Lane III.

[25] The investment advisers hired to value the assets of the Maiden Lane facilities had to determine the fair value of the securities by using valuation models that were based on uncertain projections of future cash flows and the operative discount rate. The securities had become highly illiquid: Very few transactions—and their accompanying prices—were available for comparison, and the prices that were observed showed substantial volatility.

[26] Libor is the London interbank offered rate, an indication of the interest rate at which banks borrow unsecured funds from other banks in the London interbank market. The rates are published for different loan maturities and used as benchmarks for rates on interbank loans worldwide.

[27] In general, an economic subsidy can exist even though a program has positive net income if the costs that are used to determine net income are not comprehensive. The conceptual issues surrounding estimates of economic subsidies for credit are described in Congressional Budget Office, *Estimating the Value of Subsidies for Federal Loans and Loan Guarantees* (August 2004).

[28] A fuller explanation of the market risk premium and how it affects the price of assets and their expected returns can be found in any standard textbook on corporate finance. See, for example, Chapter 9 in Richard A. Brealey, Stewart C. Myers, and Franklin Allen, *Principles of Corporate Finance*, 9th ed. (New York: McGraw Hill/Irwin, 2008).

[29] See, for example, Congressional Budget Office, *The Troubled Asset Relief Program: Report on Transactions Through December 31, 2008*. Discounting expected future cash flows to the present with a discount rate that takes into account the market risk premium is a common approach to estimating the fair value of a financial asset.

[30] On April 2, 2009, the Financial Accounting Standards Board voted to revise its Statement of Financial Accounting Standards No. 157 to account for fair value calculations when a market is inactive. The effect of the revision is that in such circumstances, banks have more leeway to use their own judgment to determine whether an asset has suffered a decline in its fair value.

[31] No upper bounds were set on lending through the Primary Dealer Credit Facility, the Commercial Paper Funding Facility, or the Asset Backed Commercial Paper Money Market Mutual Fund Liquidity Facility. Caps of $540 billion and $200 billion were placed on lending through the Money Market Investor Funding Facility and the Term Asset Backed Securities Loan Facility, respectively. (For additional detail, see Appendix A.) Lending in support of specific institutions was initially $85 billion for AIG, $220 billion for Citigroup, and $87 billion for Bank of America.

[32] The interest rates that the Federal Reserve received on the swaps were determined in competitive auctions whose participants were the private foreign banks.

[33] The primary credit rate is the interest rate at which an eligible depository institution may borrow funds, typically for a short period, directly from the discount window at a Federal Reserve Bank.

[34] Considerable variation can be found in the quality of the securities within a rating class, including the class that comprises highly rated commercial paper. Variation was even greater during the crisis, when the financial condition of issuers of the paper was changing rapidly.

[35] The interest rate on the paper being purchased was the three month overnight indexed swap rate plus 1 percentage point (for unsecured paper) and 3 percentage points (for asset backed paper). (The three month overnight indexed swap rate is a mea sure of the average federal funds rate that market participants expect over the next three months.) There was also a surcharge of 1 percentage point on unsecured paper, and each borrower paid a facility fee equal to 10 basis points (a basis point is one hundredth of a percentage point) of the maximum amount of its commercial paper that the CPFF might own.

[36] The impact of the Federal Reserve's purchases in the market is analogous to the impact of foreign official purchases in the market for U.S. Treasury debt. A study that found evidence suggesting that those foreign purchases had a large effect on the prices of Treasury securities was Ben S. Bernanke, Brian P. Sack, and Vin cent R. Reinhart, "Monetary Policy Alternatives at the Zero Bound: An Empirical Assessment," *Brookings Papers on Economic Activity,* no. 2 (2004). The impact on prices in the bond markets from large sized transactions and a high frequency of purchases was examined by Michael Fleming in "Measuring Treasury Market Liquidity," *Federal Reserve Bank of New York Economic Policy Review* (September 2003), and by Michael Brandt and Kenneth Kavajecz in "Price Discovery in the U.S. Treasury Market: The Impact of Orderflow and Liquidity on the Yield Curve," *Journal of Finance*, vol. 59, no. 6 (December 2004).

[37] Further information about the law is available at www. federalreserve.gov/ aboutthefed/ fract.htm.

[38] The Federal Reserve can increase liquidity in a market—essentially make it easier to convert assets to cash—by standing ready to buy securities or to lend against them as collateral.

[39] Monetary policy comprises the actions of a central bank to influence the availability and cost of money and credit as a means of helping to promote the goals of maximum employment, stable prices, and moderate long term interest rates. The traditional tools of monetary policy include open market operations, direct lending to depository institutions, and reserve requirements for certain deposit liabilities of depository institutions. (Reserves are an

amount of funds held back from investment by a bank to meet probable or possible demands.) For additional information, see Box 2 on page 6.

[40] See William C. Dudley, Executive Vice President, Federal Reserve Bank of New York, "May You Live in Interesting Times" (remarks at the Federal Reserve Bank of Philadelphia, October 17, 2007).

[41] As the financial crisis subsided, the Federal Reserve has begun to normalize the terms for borrowing from the discount window. The maximum term of primary credit loans—loans to generally sound depository institutions—from the discount window fell to 28 days in January 2010 and to overnight in March (before the crisis, the typical term for such credit). In addition, in February of this year, the Federal Reserve raised the interest rate on primary credit from 0.5 percent to 0.75 percent.

[42] Primary dealers—commercial banks as well as brokers and dealers in securities who buy and sell U.S. government and other securities in the private financial markets—trade with the Federal Reserve. Such firms must meet requirements set by the central bank for liquidity and capital as well as for other aspects of their operations.

[43] A mortgage backed security is a claim on the cash flows of a pool of mortgages. In this context, the "agencies" are Fannie Mae, Fred die Mac, Ginnie Mae, and the Federal Home Loan Banks. All of those entities issue debt to fund their operations, and all but the Federal Home Loan Banks guarantee mortgage backed securities.

[44] Federal Reserve Bank of New York, *Domestic Open Market Opera tions During 2008: A Report Prepared for the Federal Open Market Committee by the Markets Group of the Federal Reserve Bank of New York* (January 2009), p. 11, footnote 7, available at www. newyorkfed.org/markets/omo/omo2008.pdf.

[45] Board of Governors of the Federal Reserve System, *Monetary Policy Report to the Congress* (February 24, 2009), p. 48, available at www.federalreserve.gov/ monetarypolicy/ files/ 20090224_ mprfullreport.pdf.

[46] Those banks were the Reserve Bank of Australia, the Banco Central do Brasil, the Bank of Canada, the Danmarks Nationalbank, the Bank of Korea, the Bank of Mexico, the Reserve Bank of New Zealand, Norway's Norges Bank, the Monetary Authority of Singapore, and Sweden's Sveriges Riksbank.

[47] The Federal Reserve has indicated that the TAF could become a permanent addition to its tools for implementing monetary policy.

[48] In contrast, primary credit is available on a very short term basis, typically overnight.

[49] The last auction was on March 8, 2010, and the minimum rate was 0.5 percent, up from the previous minimum of 0.25 percent.

[50] For more information on the repo market, see Tobias Adrian, Christopher R. Burke, and James J. McAndrews, "The Federal Reserve's Primary Dealer Credit Facility," *Current Issues in Economics and Finance*, Federal Reserve Bank of New York, vol. 15, no. 4 (August 2009); and Peter Hördahl and Michael R. King, "Developments in Repo Markets During the Financial Turmoil," *BIS Quarterly Review* (Bank for International Settlements, December 2008), pp. 37–53.

[51] The TSLF is an expanded version of the SOMA (System Open Market Account) securities lending program that the Federal Reserve has offered since 2002. That program provides primary dealers with overnight loans of particularly sought after Treasury securities in exchange for other Treasury securities as collateral. Just before the TSLF was created, lending under the SOMA securities lending program averaged about $15 billion.

[52] The two types of auctions were known as Schedule 1 and Schedule 2. In the first, loans could be collateralized by Treasury securities, agency debt, and agency MBSs; in the second, they could be backed by the collateral eligible for Schedule 1 auction loans as well as by highly rated corporate, municipal, mortgage backed, and asset backed securities.

[53] Money market mutual funds are a significant source of short term funding for financial institutions as well as for some corporations and government entities. For investors, the

funds are an alternative to bank deposits: They pay a slightly higher rate of interest, but they expose investors to greater risk because they are not insured.

[54] In addition, on September 29, the Treasury began a temporary guarantee program, funded under the Troubled Asset Relief Program, to protect shareholders of money market mutual funds from losses. The program ended as scheduled on September 18, 2009.

[55] A bank holding company is broadly defined as any company that has control over a bank. Becoming a bank holding company pro vides a corporate and legal status that in many cases brings greater financial flexibility and makes it easier for banks to raise capital.

[56] The temporary increase in May in the amount borrowed through the AMLF occurred at about the time of the release of the results of the Federal Reserve's Supervisory Capital Assessment Program (commonly known as the bank stress tests), which measured the adequacy of the capital of major financial institutions. See Board of Governors of the Federal Reserve System, *Federal Reserve System Monthly Report on Credit and Liquidity Programs and the Balance Sheet* (June 2009), available at www.federalreserve.gov/ monetarypolicy/files/monthlyclbsreport200906.pdf.

[57] Institutions that were eligible to sell assets to the SPVs included money market funds and other investors in the money markets, such as U.S. based securities lenders and investment funds that operate in a manner similar to money market funds—for example, certain local government investment pools, common trust funds, and collective investment funds.

[58] See Board of Governors of the Federal Reserve System, "2008 Monetary Policy Releases: October 7, 2008" (press release), available at www.federalreserve.gov/ newsevents/ press/ monetary/ 20081007c.htm.

[59] The three month overnight indexed swap rate is a measure of the average federal funds rate that market participants expect over the next three months.

[60] The maximum amount of a single issuer's commercial paper that the CPFF might own at any time was the greatest amount of U.S. dollar denominated commercial paper that the issuer had outstanding on any day between January 1 and August 31, 2008. Once the total amount of an issuer's outstanding commercial paper held by all investors (including the CPFF) equaled or exceeded the issuer's limit, the CPFF would not purchase additional commercial paper from that issuer. See www. newyorkfed.org/markets/cpff_terms_conditions.html.

[61] See Board of Governors of the Federal Reserve System, *Federal Reserve System Monthly Report on Credit and Liquidity Programs and the Balance Sheet*, p. 9.

[62] The Federal Reserve announced in February 2009 (see www. federalreserve.gov/ monetarypolicy/20090210b.htm) that it was prepared to increase the size of the program to as much as $1 trillion.

[63] Floorplan loans include revolving lines of credit to finance the inventories of motor vehicle dealers. Insurance premium finance loans include loans originated for the purpose of paying premiums on property and casualty insurance; they do not include deferred payment obligations acquired from insurance companies. Eligible mortgage servicing advance receivables include receivables created by principal and interest, tax and insurance, and corporate advances made by residential mortgage servicers approved by Fannie Mae or Freddie Mac under pooling and servicing agreements or similar servicing agreements. For more information, see www.newyorkfed.org/markets/talf_terms.html.

[64] Five year terms may be used for loans secured by Small Business Administration (SBA) Pool Certificates or by SBA Development Company Participation Certificates, or for securities backed by student loans or commercial mortgage loans.

[65] Fannie Mae and Freddie Mac were originally created as federally chartered institutions but were privately owned and operated. Designed to facilitate the flow of investment funds to the housing market, they pool mortgages purchased from mortgage lenders and sell them as mortgage backed securities, collecting annual guarantee fees on the mortgages they securitize. In return, Fannie Mae and Freddie Mac cover any losses that occur if the underlying mortgage loans default. The companies also hold mortgage loans in their

portfolios and purchase mortgage backed securities (their own or those of other institutions), from which they earn a return.

[66] The Federal Home Loan Banks are government sponsored enterprises that lending institutions use to obtain low cost financing through "advances," which are loans backed by high quality col lateral. Ginnie Mae is a government owned corporation that guarantees securities backed by federally insured loans—mainly loans insured by the Federal Housing Administration and the Department of Veterans Affairs.

[67] The Treasury issues notes with maturities that range from 2 to 10 years and bonds with maturities of 30 years. (At the end of July 2007, the Federal Reserve also held more than $277 billion in short term Treasury bills.)

[68] The Federal Reserve extended a loan of $13 billion through the discount window to JPMorgan Chase on March 14, 2008. That loan was repaid three days later with almost $4 million of interest.

[69] An LLC offers protection from personal liability for business debts, just as a corporation does. The profits and losses of the business pass through to its owners, as they would if the business were a partnership or sole proprietorship.

[70] For a detailed explanation of AIG's financial problems, see William K. Sjostrom Jr., "The AIG Bailout," *Washington and Lee Law Review,* vol. 66 (November 1, 2009), available at http:// papers.ssrn.com/sol3/papers.cfm?abstract_id=1346552.

[71] As of November 5, 2008 AIG had approximately $61 billion outstanding under the line of credit and $19.9 billion in outstanding advances under the Securities Borrowing Facility. See Board of Governors of the Federal Reserve System, *Report Pursuant to Section 129 of the Emergency Economic Stabilization Act of 2008: Restructuring of the Government's Financial Support to the American International Group, Inc., on November 10, 2008,* available at www.federalreserve.gov/monetarypolicy/files/ 129aigrestructure.pdf.

[72] Each discount rate reflects a premium over the rate on a Treasury security that accounts for the "market risk" associated with the programs—the risk that losses will be largest when the economy is weak and the economic cost of the losses is greatest.

[73] The maturity of the collateral (the commercial paper) for such borrowing may extend in some cases to 270 days, but because shorter loan terms are more common for commercial paper, CBO assumed that the average maturity backing the loans was 90 days. Assuming a longer (or shorter) maturity would increase (or decrease) the estimated subsidy.

[74] The rate charged by the Federal Reserve depends on whether the commercial paper serving as collateral is backed by assets. The rate is set at a spread over the three month overnight indexed swap rate, which is closely related to other overnight bank rates, such as the federal funds rate and the overnight Libor rate.

[75] CBO modeled those cash flows using an expected net charge off rate (loan losses minus recoveries, as a percentage of outstanding loans) each period that was consistent with its economic forecast.

INDEX

A

B

C

D

E

F

M

N

O

P

R

S